Lectionary Worship Workbook

Series V
Cycle A

D.J. Dent / Linda R. Holcombe

G

Copyright © 2016 by
CSS Publishing Company, Inc.
Lima, Ohio

Scripture quotations are from the New Revised Standard Version of the Bible, copyright 1989 by the Division of Christian Education of the National Council of the Churches of God in the USA. Used by permission.

For more information about CSS Publishing Company resources, visit our website at www.csspub.com or email us at csr@csspub.com or call (800) 241-4056.

ISSN: 1938-5560

e-book
ISBN-13: 978-0-7880-2855-7
ISBN-10: 0-7880-2855-3

ISBN-13: 978-0-7880-2854-0
ISBN-10: 0-7880-2854-5

PRINTED IN USA

Table Of Contents

Introduction

This book has been a revelation to me for a number of reasons. Perhaps the most significant is a detailed recognition of the beauty of the lectionary. I do not mean this in a pandering sense of agreement (so that I can get my appropriate gold star for being a good team player), but as a new appreciation for the efforts of those who crafted and forged the readings contained therein. Their desire to tell a unified story across a few weeks or a season is commendable and inspirational. This book is an attempt to honor that tradition. Its value is contained less in a single phrase, but more in the concepts and shared ideas spanning several weeks and sometimes months.

No shortage of words is used by the preacher to try and remind the people that Advent is not Christmas. We have tried to create within the words and movements of the liturgies of the church year a feel and theme that fit and enhance the intended meaning of the day. If a tight enough narrative can be woven, perhaps the message can be delivered clearly and possibly with a new meaning that any individual or community had not encountered before.

It is in this hope that we humbly offer this book to your reading and reflection. You may use it as an end if you find it fills exactly what you were looking for, but hopefully it also encourages the freedom to explore and create unique portions for your community. After all, the Spirit does move in strange ways.

+ Pastor DJ Dent

Some Tips On Use

The construction of most of the liturgies depends heavily on the *Western (or Roman) Rite*. If there is a proposed variance from this formula in one of the liturgies, all of the liturgical pieces are laid out in order. If you are of a tradition that does not typically follow this pattern in worship, there are two considerations for you:

1) We would encourage at least a cursory attempt to step through this formal, structured liturgy, at least for a period of time to see how or even if it fits. An appendix exists on page 9 with a brief explanation of each of the parts of the liturgy.

2) The words and prayers do not necessarily need to be restricted to these particular moments in worship, but the language and prayers could be expanded and used elsewhere — or without formal structure at all.

The shorthand in each of the liturgies is as follows:
P is the pastor or presiding minister.
A is the assisting minister (usually a layperson).
C is always bolded and is the congregational response.
L is rarely used, but refers to the lector or reader.
+ is a marker for where the symbol of the cross should be traced as a blessing.

Occasionally, there are proposed alternative texts. These mean no disrespect to the lectionary, but are submitted because they fit within the broader theme of the season, and provide additional opportunity to reflect on God's word alongside the other lectionary readings. For instance, in Advent, there are readings about preparation and watchfulness. In the theme alternative text, these same ideas are present, but in a way that ties closer to the specific theme for the day. If you would prefer to ignore these, the themes will still fit, but perhaps not as smoothly.

There are also helpful items to remember, including national holidays and lesser festivals in the church year. Commemorations were left out because of the differences between denominational bodies, but the lesser festivals were left in case you wanted to make mention of a particular saint in remembrance during the prayers or in the sermon.

Music In Worship — Lectionary Workbook A

Music is essential to worship, and plays an integral role in setting the tone for the entire worship experience for your congregation. All of the traditional hymns and contemporary songs that are listed in this workbook have been successfully used in worship multiple times, and will assist you in creating cohesive worship for all involved.

The traditional hymns are cited from six different sources, and intentionally include Lutheran, United Methodist, Presbyterian, and Episcopal hymnals. If you do not have access to these hymnals in hard copy form, you will find these hymns online at www.hymnary.org. This website is a comprehensive resource for literally hundreds of hymns and hymnals, and is an excellent tool for use in planning music for worship.

List Of Hymnals Used In This Workbook By Date Published And Their Abbreviations

GG — *Glory To God—The Presbyterian Hymnal*, Louisville, Presbyterian Publishing Corporation, 2013.

ELW — *Evangelical Lutheran Worship*, Minneapolis, Augsburg Fortress Publishers, 2006.

WOV — *With One Voice*, Minneapolis, Augsburg Fortress Publishers, 1995.

UMH — *The United Methodist Hymnal*, Nashville, United Methodist Publishing House, 1989.

H – *The Hymnal 1982, Episcopal Church in the USA*, New York, Published by Church Publishing Incorporated, 1985.

LBW — *Lutheran Book Of Worship*, Minneapolis, Augsburg Fortress Publishers, 1978.

The contemporary songs used in this Lectionary Workbook are cited from several online sources where you will find access to printable Lead Sheets, full SATB vocal arrangements, lyrics, options for transposing the song into the ideal key for your situation, and recordings of the songs. Finding worship/praise music online is the most efficient way to support your contemporary music ministry, as you can locate just about any song you're looking for, and you can customize the music.

List Of Online Sources Used In This Workbook For Contemporary Music

www.ccli.com
Christian Copyright Licensing International is an important organization to belong to for access to tons of CCM (Contemporary Christian Music) titles and Lead Sheets for a lot less money. Your church can purchase an annual CCLI license and SongSelect (cost is based on the size of your congregation), and then you have unlimited access to downloadable lead sheets and lyrics, sample recordings, and more. You can also purchase rehearsal licenses (for when you need to distribute audio files of music to band members for listening and easier learning), video licenses (for when you need to show video clips or films in any area of your church ministry), and streaming licenses (for when you want to stream your services online and do it legally).

www.praisecharts.com
An excellent site for finding CCM songs and very detailed lead sheets and full scores. You do have to pay

to purchase each song, but you can also purchase certain numbers of downloads within a year for a single fee that's ultimately cheaper.

www.musicnotes.com
A great site for getting very current sheet music…this site often has songs that CCLI and praisecharts do not have when you need something very current. This is also a pay-per-song site.

www.dakotaroadmusic.com
Great site for beginning contemporary worship bands. Dakota Road is also an excellent resource for more contemporary liturgical songs that can be used as a Kyrie, Gospel Welcome, Offertory, or Lamb of God in your worship services. This is also a pay-per-song site.

I wish you all the best in your worship planning, and please don't hesitate to contact me if I can be of further assistance in any way.

Linda Holcombe, MMEd
Director of Music
Christ Lutheran Church, Highlands Ranch, CO
lholcombe@clchr.org
303-791-0803, ext. 109 (CLC Music)

Parts Of The Liturgy

Invocation

An invitation for God to be present. Traditionally, this is simply "In the name of the Father, and of the Son, and of the Holy Spirit." It is meant to offer a moment to prepare for the arrival of God, and is typically accompanied by the sign of the cross being made either by the pastor/presiding minister or the individual worshiper, or both.

Confession And Forgiveness

We primarily receive God's grace through the forgiveness of sins, and confession should always accompany forgiveness. This is omitted in the Easter season as a sign of the power of the resurrection.

Kyrie

Literally, "Lord" from the Latin. This is a petition for God's help. It is not changed in any liturgies in this book, but typically follows the formula "Lord, have mercy."

Hymn Of Praise

Accompanies the Kyrie as thanksgiving for God's response to our plea for mercy. This can be omitted during Lent and Advent to provide a sense of longing for God's work.

Apostolic Greeting

Usually found at the beginning of Paul's letters, the traditional formula is "The grace of our Lord Jesus Christ, the love of God, and the communion of the Holy Spirit be with you always" while the congregation responds with "And also with you." It is a way of greeting one another in the name of Christ.

Prayer Of The Day

A way of summing up the readings of the day in the form of a prayer. Each of these is built around the lectionary and/or the alternative texts for the given day.

Reading Of The Word

The church is the congregation where the word is proclaimed, and the sacraments are administered rightly (a modification from Article 7 of the Augsburg Confession, also known as the beliefs of the reformers). Reading of God's word should occur at every worship.

Sermon

Should be a proclamation of the good news.

Creed

Literally, "I believe" from the Latin. Traditionally the Church adheres to three creeds: Nicene, Apostles, and Athanasian. These are statements of faith that unite the church across time and space.

Prayers Of The Church

Also called the Prayers Of Intercession, these are the moments in the liturgy when all petitions are raised to God on behalf of others. Typically, these include illnesses, struggles, deaths, and other challenges, but can also include joys and celebrations. They also typically include praying for specific instances and people in our world who need support and guidance.

Offertory Prayer

A way of blessing the offering that is given. A prayer that usually acknowledges that these things are already God's, but we want to ask God's blessing as they are being given back.

Proper Preface

A prayer that precedes the Words of Institution. It acknowledges the many ways God has acted in the world, and prepares the congregation for the singing of the Sanctus.

Sanctus

Traditionally, from Isaiah 6:3 and Matthew 21:9, "Holy, holy, holy Lord, God of power and might, heaven and earth are full of your glory. Hosanna in the highest. Blessed is He who comes in the name of the Lord. Hosanna in the highest." This can be sung or spoken and is referred to as the saints' unending hymn.

Words Of Institution

The words spoken over the bread and wine at Communion. "For I received from the Lord what I also delivered to you, that the Lord Jesus on the night when he was betrayed took bread, and when he had given thanks, he broke it, and said, 'This is my body which is for you. Do this in remembrance of me.' In the same way also he took the cup, after supper, saying, 'This cup is the new covenant in my blood. Do this, as often as you drink it, in remembrance of me.' For as often as you eat this bread and drink the cup, you proclaim the Lord's death until he comes." The Lutherans and Anglicans have slight variations of this same blessing.

Communion Welcome

Not usually a formal part of the Western Rite, but an invitation to the people of God to come forward for the meal.

Post-Communion Blessing

A blessing from the pastor/presiding minister that the elements of Communion achieve their purpose in the bodies of those who have communed.

Post-Communion Prayer

A prayer by those who communed, who ask for the blessings of Communion.

Benediction

A blessing from the pastor/presiding minister as a final offering on the faithful for what has happened in the worship.

Dismissal

A sending and final word on the worship.

Stated simply, Advent is a direct transliteration of the Latin word "Adventus," meaning "coming." In the liturgical calendar, it occupies the four Sundays preceding Christmas Day on December 25. Its history involves the retelling of the stories of the anticipation of the Messiah, and especially the prominence and proclamation of John the Baptist as the voice of one "calling out in the wilderness" to prepare the pathway for God entering the world through Jesus. The complexity and the magnitude of the divine becoming human surpass our ability to understand.

For the sake of this book, Advent, Christmas, and Epiphany are held together, then, to form an overarching theme. Many expectations were placed on the coming Messiah to heal the hurts of the world. Rather than list or lament over the multitude of dark places, one particular theme is chosen, which in itself is rich and deep and could be mined in any number of ways. The title given to this theme is "Good N.E.W.S. Dawning." Here, the acronym "N.E.W.S." stands for North, East, West, and South. The subtext to the title includes two main ideas, 1) that God calls us from all directions on Earth to anticipate and worship Christ, and 2) that, in essence, we are wandering until we find our home in Christ. During Advent, these two subtexts are explored in anticipation of our Christmas celebration when the good news arrives in the form of the Christ child. Epiphany continues this theme by offering gifts at the arrival of the Christ child. There is a musical selection included to be used as a theme song for the season of Advent; it is recommended as a conclusion to the litany where the Advent wreath is lit.

The recommended readings for the season, labeled "Theme Alternative Texts," are consistent with the traditional themes of Advent. These can be used in tandem, as a replacement for RCL texts, in supplement, or ignored altogether. The theme works as a particular topic in which to acknowledge the need for a messiah and thus ties in with the traditional readings.

Each week in Advent corresponds to one of the cardinal directions on a compass. The recommendation for any type of children's sermon would be to investigate what the kids think of when they hear "North" or any of the other directions. For example, we affiliate "North" with "cold" or "snow." The leaders are commended to then offer their thoughts for affiliations and reflect on how God speaks to those ideas.

For proclamation, the same can be done by the pastor. To make the sermon as concrete and engaging as possible, it is recommended that whoever is preaching gather a single idea or image from the cardinal direction for the day, and then discuss it in concert with Christmas or Advent themes. An example would be the standard "Christmas Tree" as an idea and how the conical evergreen is mostly a northern phenomenon, which could lead into a discussion about Christmas trees in other areas of the world in an attempt at bridging cultural gaps.

For prayers, specific petitions tying us to the region for the day are recommended. If there is a significant issue facing "northern" countries, for instance, those should be included as part of the intercessory prayers. For unique decoration, there should be a mobile, prominent piece that is moved to a different area for each week. Either, for the week of the North, you place the decoration to the North of the chancel area if there is a freestanding altar present, or the northernmost place in the nave. The other weeks would beg the decoration to correspond to the theme.

Recommended is an Epiphany star attached to the top of a pole or suspended from the ceiling if possible. If either is prohibitive, moving an Advent Wreath or Crucifix would suffice. If using the Epiphany star, it is recommended to actually place it opposite the cardinal direction for the day. The logic for this is if we are celebrating/remembering the North, the Epiphany star would draw us to the center, which would mean leading us South. In practice, people may not be spatially aware enough, and this would cause cognitive dissonance. Simplicity in explaining the symbol reigns here, so do whichever communicates the clearest. An idea for construction of the star would be to build one from wire frame and gold fabric, or purchase one of large stature at a local Christmas store. It can be easily affixed with tape atop a section of PVC pipe. The base can be a simple wood block with a hole drilled to fit the pipe. The star should be gold and the pipe and base painted to match.

Advent 1

Advent Theme direction: North
Traditional Theme: Hope

Texts
Isaiah 2:1-5
Psalm 122
Romans 13:11-14
Matthew 24:36-44

Theme Alternative Texts
Isaiah 61:1-3
Mark 13:24-37

Music Of The Day-Advent Theme Music *(For Traditional, Blended, or Contemporary Worship)*
"Good News Dawning" by Linda Holcombe (Advent Gathering/Opening Song/Hymn)
"Shout To The North" by Martin Smith with Advent lyrics by Linda Holcombe (Advent Gospel Welcome)

Music Of The Day Traditional Hymns
"O Come, O Come, Emmanuel" (ELW257, GG88, UMH211, H56)
"Prepare The Royal Highway/Prepare The Way, O Zion" (ELW 264, GG106, LBW26, H65)
"Soon And Very Soon" (ELW 439, GG384, UMH706)
"Creator Of The Stars Of Night" (ELW 245, GG84, UMH692, H60)
"The King Shall Come" (ELW 260, LBW33, H73)
"People Look East" (ELW248, GG105, UMH202, WOV626)

Music Of The Day Contemporary Songs
"Messiah" by Larry Olson (Dakota Road Music)
"Sing To The King" by Foote/Horne (ccli.com SongSelect)
"Glory To The King" by Darlene Zschech (ccli.com SongSelect)
"Prepare The Way" by Hall/Giglio (ccli.com SongSelect)

Important Items
The festival for Saint Andrew is on November 30.

Invocation
P   Blessed be our Lord, + God of the North, East, West, and South, who draws us to reconciliation through Christ.
C   **Amen.**

Confession And Forgiveness

P   Let us return to God, confessing where we have wandered.

(pause for meditation and reflection)

P   God of all,

C   **we confess that we have left your guidance. We have distanced ourselves from you and our family by our action and our inaction. Grant us your mercy, that we may be brought back to you and to the entire creation.**

P   Brothers and sisters in Christ, no matter how far you stray, you are welcome home. By the mercy of God + your sins are forgiven. May you live refreshed in the warm embrace of God our Father.

C   **Amen.**

Litany Of The Advent Wreath

P   We praise you, God of hope, for this evergreen crown

C   **that marks our preparation for Christ.**

   (Acolyte moves to light first candle)

P   The light of this candle leads us from the darkness

C   **to a place in your warm embrace, safe from the cold.**

P   May our hearts be melted to reach out in hope;

C   **wake our minds to a new way of being.**

P   Grant this through Christ our Lord,

C   **whose day draws ever near. Amen.**

(sing "Good N.E.W.S. Dawning")

Apostolic Greeting

P   Grace and peace be yours from God, who calls you through the darkness and into the light.

C   **Amen.**

Prayer Of The Day

A   Let us pray. Draw us into your kingdom, Lord;

C   **by your mercy, remove our apathy from us. May your spirit keep us awake and draw us from our own prejudices to believe that your good news is for all. Amen.**

Prayers Of The Church

A   Let us pray for those unsettled, those wrestling, those lost, and for all in need:

(The prayers should include petitions this week for areas and nations considered northern and whatever current issues they face.)

(After each petition)

A   By your grace, O Lord,

C   **hear us as we call.**

A Hear our voices, and draw near to those who need your presence, granting peace, wholeness, and all else we need, through Jesus Christ our Lord.

C **Amen.**

Offertory Prayer

A Let us pray. God of grace,

C **we return to you what you have entrusted to us. May you bless these gifts and all that we are to the care of all in need, until the return of your Son, our Savior and Lord. Amen.**

Proper Preface

P It is right to give praise to you, God our Father, through our Lord Jesus Christ. For you reach into the void and mold us into your creation. We give thanks; for your breath gives life and moves through us, lifting our voices alongside those saints of all times and places to join in their unending hymn. *(Sanctus spoken or sung)*

Communion Welcome

P Come to the table; be fed and united in the body and blood of Christ.

Post-Communion Blessing

P May the body and blood of Jesus Christ carry you in your vocation, and keep your heart filled with mercy.

C **Amen.**

Post-Communion Prayer

A Let us pray. Lord God,

C **we give thanks that you have brought the good news to us once again in your body and blood. As we are joined in this meal once again with you, may we stretch the bounds of your family, bringing home all who are scattered. Amen.**

Benediction

P May God shield you in your trials, may Christ + strengthen you for each day, and may the Spirit light your path on your journey.

C **Amen.**

Dismissal

A Go in peace, seek the lost, bring them home.

C **Thanks be to God.**

Advent 2

Advent Theme Direction: East
Traditional Theme: Love

Texts
Isaiah 11:1-10
Psalm 72:1-7, 18-19
Romans 15:4-13
Matthew 3:1-12

Theme Alternative Texts
Isaiah 52:7-10
Mark 1:1-8

Music Of The Day—Advent Theme Music *(For Traditional, Blended, or Contemporary Worship)*
"Good News Dawning" by Linda Holcombe (Advent Gathering/Opening Song/Hymn)
"Shout To The North" by Martin Smith with Advent lyrics by Linda Holcombe (Advent Gospel Welcome)

Music Of The Day Traditional Hymns
"On Jordan's Banks The Baptist's Cry" (ELW249, GG96, LBW36, H76)
"Light One Candle To Watch For Messiah" (ELW240, GG85)
"O Come, O Come, Emmanuel" (ELW257, GG88, UMH211, H56)
"Prepare The Royal Highway/Prepare The Way, O Zion" (ELW 264, GG106, LBW26, H65)
"People Look East" (ELW248, GG105, UMH202, WOV626)

Music Of The Day Contemporary Songs
"Days Of Elijah" by Robin Mark (ccli.com SongSelect)
"Jesus Messiah" by Carson/Tomlin/Cash/Reeves (ccli.com SongSelect)
"Open Up The Heavens" by Meredith Andrews (ccli.com SongSelect)
"Prepare The Way" by Hall/Giglio (ccli.com SongSelect)

Invocation
P   Blessed be our Lord, + God of the North, East, West, and South, who draws us to reconciliation through Christ.
C   **Amen.**

Confession And Forgiveness
P   Let us return to God, confessing where we have wandered.
(pause for meditation and reflection)

P   God of all,

C   **we confess that we have left your guidance. We have distanced ourselves from you and our family by our action and our inaction. Grant us your mercy, that we may be brought back to you and to the entire creation.**

P   Brothers and sisters in Christ, no matter how far you stray, you are welcome home. By the mercy of God, + your sins are forgiven. May you live refreshed in the warm embrace of God our Father.

C   **Amen.**

Litany Of The Advent Wreath

P   We praise you, God of love, for this evergreen crown

C   **that marks our preparation for Christ.**

(Acolyte moves to light first and second candles)

P   The light of this candle leads us from loneliness

C   **to a family larger than we can imagine.**

P   May we gaze upon the stars in peace,

C   **knowing that we, too, have our place.**

P   Grant this through Christ our Lord,

C   **whose day draws ever near. Amen.**

(sing "Good N.E.W.S. Dawning")

Apostolic Greeting

P   Grace and peace be yours from God, who calls you through the darkness and into the light.

C   **Amen.**

Prayer Of The Day

A   Let us pray. Draw us into your kingdom, Lord.

C   **By Your grace, wake us to the good news. May we find ways to be reconnected to all things; and help us preach the story of reconciliation and peace to all of our neighbors; we pray this through Jesus Christ our Lord. Amen.**

Prayers Of The Church

A   Let us pray for those unsettled, those wrestling, those lost, and for all in need:

(The prayers should include petitions this week for areas and nations considered eastern and whatever current issues they face.)

(After each petition)

A   By your grace, O Lord,

C   **hear us as we call.**

A   Hear our voices, and draw near to those who need your presence, granting peace, wholeness, and all else we need, through Jesus Christ our Lord.

C   **Amen.**

Offertory Prayer

A Let us pray. God of grace,

C **we return to you what you have entrusted to us. May you bless these gifts and all that we are to the care of all in need, until the return of your Son, our Savior and Lord. Amen.**

Proper Preface

P It is right to give praise to you, God our Father, through our Lord Jesus Christ. For you reach into the void and mold us into your creation. We give thanks for your breath gives life and moves through us, lifting our voices alongside those saints of all times and places to join in their unending hymn. *(Sanctus spoken or sung)*

Communion Welcome

P Come to the table; be fed and united in the body and blood of Christ.

Post-Communion Blessing

P May the body and blood of Jesus Christ carry you in your vocation, and keep your heart filled with mercy.

C **Amen.**

Post-Communion Prayer

A Let us pray. Lord God,

C **we give thanks that you have brought the good news to us once again in your body and blood. As we are joined in this meal once again with you, may we stretch the bounds of your family, bringing home all who are scattered. Amen.**

Benediction

P May God shield you in your trials, may Christ + strengthen you for each day, and may the Spirit light your path on your journey.

C **Amen.**

Dismissal

A Go in peace, seek the lost, bring them home.

C **Thanks be to God.**

Advent 3

Advent Theme Direction: West
Traditional Theme: Joy

Texts
Isaiah 35:1-10
Psalm 146:5-10 alt (Luke 1:46b-55)
James 5:7-10
Matthew 11:2-11

Theme Alternative Texts
Psalm 98
John 1:6-8, 19-28

Music Of The Day-Advent Theme Music *(For Traditional, Blended, or Contemporary Worship)*
"Good News Dawning" by Linda Holcombe (Advent Gathering/Opening Song/Hymn)
"Shout To The North" by Martin Smith with Advent lyrics by Linda Holcombe (Advent Gospel Welcome)

Music Of The Day Traditional Hymns
"He Came Down" (ELW 253, GG137)
"Rejoice, Rejoice, Believers" (ELW244, GG362, LBW25, H68)
"Come, Thou Long-Expected Jesus" (ELW254, GG82, UMH196, LBW30, H66)
"The King Shall Come" (ELW 260, LBW33, H73)
"Prepare The Royal Highway/Prepare The Way, O Zion" (ELW 264, GG106, LBW26, H65)

Music Of The Day Contemporary Songs
"Prepare Ye The Way" by Tommy Walker (ccli.com SongSelect)
"Go" by Chris Christensen (ccli.com SongSelect)
"Emmanuel" by Raymond Badham (ccli.com SongSelect)
"Sing To The King" by Foote/Horne (ccli.com SongSelect)
"Prepare The Way" by Hall/Giglio (ccli.com SongSelect)

Invocation
P   Blessed be our Lord, + God of the North, East, West, and South, who draws us to reconciliation through Christ.
C   **Amen.**

Confession And Forgiveness

P   Let us return to God, confessing where we have wandered.

(pause for meditation and reflection)

P   God of all,

C   we confess that we have left your guidance. We have distanced ourselves from you and our family by our action and our inaction. Grant us your mercy, that we may be brought back to you and to the entire creation.

P   Brothers and sisters in Christ, no matter how far you stray, you are welcome home. By the mercy of God, + your sins are forgiven. May you live refreshed in the warm embrace of God our Father.

C   Amen.

Litany Of The Advent Wreath

P   We praise you, God of joy, for this evergreen crown

C   that marks our preparation for Christ.

(Acolyte moves to light first, second, and third candles)

P   The light of this candle leads us from a world without meaning

C   to symbols and stories that give us life.

P   May we joyfully wonder at the world

C   and find excitement in every facet.

P   Grant this through Christ our Lord,

C   whose day draws ever near. Amen.

(sing "Good N.E.W.S. Dawning")

Apostolic Greeting

P   Grace and peace be yours from God, who calls you through the darkness and into the light.

C   Amen.

Prayer Of The Day

A   Let us pray. Draw us into your kingdom, Lord;

C   by your grace, kindle the fire in us. Give us the passion to seek value in even the simplest and smallest parts of this creation; this we pray through Jesus Christ our Lord. Amen.

Prayers Of The Church

A   Let us pray for those unsettled, those wrestling, those lost, and for all in need:

(The prayers should include petitions this week for areas and nations considered Western and whatever current issues they face.)

(After each petition)

A   By your grace, O Lord,

C   hear us as we call.

A Hear our voices, and draw near to those who need your presence, granting peace, wholeness, and all else we need, through Jesus Christ our Lord.

C **Amen.**

Offertory Prayer

A Let us pray. God of grace,

C **we return to you what you have entrusted to us. May you bless these gifts and all that we are to the care of all in need, until the return of your Son, our Savior and Lord. Amen.**

Proper Preface

P It is right to give praise to you, God our Father, through our Lord Jesus Christ. For you reach into the void and mold us into your creation. We give thanks for your breath gives life and moves through us, lifting our voices alongside those saints of all times and places to join in their unending hymn. *(Sanctus spoken or sung)*

Communion Welcome

P Come to the table; be fed and united in the body and blood of Christ.

Post-Communion Blessing

P May the body and blood of Jesus Christ carry you in your vocation, and keep your heart filled with mercy.

C **Amen.**

Post-Communion Prayer

A Let us pray. Lord God,

C **we give thanks that you have brought the good news to us once again in your body and blood. As we are joined in this meal once again with you, may we stretch the bounds of your family, bringing home all who are scattered. Amen.**

Benediction

P May God shield you in your trials, may Christ + strengthen you for each day, and may the Spirit light your path on your journey.

C **Amen.**

Dismissal

A Go in peace, seek the lost, bring them home.

C **Thanks be to God.**

Advent 4

Advent Theme direction: South
Traditional Theme: Peace

Texts
Isaiah 7:10-16
Psalm 80:1-7, 17-19
Romans 1:1-7
Matthew 1:18-25

Theme Alternative Texts
Isaiah 40:1-11
Luke 1:26-38

Music Of The Day-Advent Theme Music *(For Traditional, Blended, or Contemporary Worship)*
"Good News Dawning" by Linda Holcombe (Advent Gathering/Opening Song/Hymn)
"Shout To The North" by Martin Smith with Advent lyrics by Linda Holcombe (Advent Gospel Welcome)

Music Of The Day Traditional Hymns
"Savior Of The Nations, Come" (ELW263, GG102, UMH214, LBW28, H54)
"Once In Royal David's City" (ELW 269)
"Lo, How A Rose E'er Blooming" (ELW272, GG129, UMH216, H81)
"Prepare The Royal Highway/Prepare The Way, O Zion" (ELW 264, GG106, LBW26, H65)
"Love Has Come" (ELW 292, GG110)

Music Of The Day Contemporary Songs
"Breath Of Heaven" by Eaton/Grant (ccli.com SongSelect)
"Mary, Did You Know?" by Greene (ccli.com SongSelect)
"Emmanuel" (Hallowed Manger Ground) by Tomlin/Cash (ccli.com SongSelect)
"He Made A Way In A Manger" by Merkel/Black (ccli.com SongSelect)
"Sing Noel" by O'Brien/Carswell (ccli.com SongSelect)
"Prepare The Way" by Hall/Giglio (ccli.com SongSelect)

Invocation
P   Blessed be our Lord, + God of the North, East, West, and South, who draws us to reconciliation through Christ.
C   Amen.

Confession And Forgiveness

P   Let us return to God, confessing where we have wandered.

(pause for meditation and reflection)

P   God of all,

C   **we confess that we have left your guidance. We have distanced ourselves from you and our family by our action and our inaction. Grant us your mercy, that we may be brought back to you and to the entire creation.**

P   Brothers and sisters in Christ, no matter how far you stray, you are welcome home. By the mercy of God, + your sins are forgiven. May you live refreshed in the warm embrace of God our Father.

C   **Amen.**

Litany Of The Advent Wreath

P   We praise you, God of peace, for this evergreen crown

C   **that marks our preparation for Christ.**

(Acolyte moves to light first, second, third, and fourth candles)

P   The light of this candle leads us from wandering

C   **to a direction and a destination.**

P   Guide us by your love;

C   **and give us focus and devotion.**

P   Grant this through Christ our Lord,

C   **whose day draws ever near. Amen.**

(sing "Good N.E.W.S. Dawning")

Apostolic Greeting

P   Grace and peace be yours from God, who calls you through the darkness and into the light.

C   **Amen.**

Prayer Of The Day

A   Let us pray. Draw us into your kingdom, Lord;

C   **by Your grace, calm our minds and our hearts. When the oceans rage and the mountains tremble, make us into your voice of calm for those around us; this we pray through Jesus Christ our Lord. Amen.**

Prayers Of The Church

A   Let us pray for those unsettled, those wrestling, those lost, and for all in need:

(The prayers should include petitions this week for areas and nations considered southern and whatever current issues they face.)

(After each petition)

A   By your grace, O Lord,

C   **hear us as we call.**

A   Hear our voices, and draw near to those who need your presence, granting peace, wholeness, and all else we need, through Jesus Christ our Lord.

C Amen.

Offertory Prayer

A Let us pray. God of grace,

C we return to you what you have entrusted to us. May you bless these gifts and all that we are to the care of all in need, until the return of your Son, our Savior and Lord. Amen.

Proper Preface

P It is right to give praise to you, God our Father, through our Lord Jesus Christ. For you reach into the void and mold us into your creation. We give thanks for your breath gives life and moves through us, lifting our voices alongside those saints of all times and places to join in their unending hymn. *(Sanctus spoken or sung)*

Communion Welcome

P Come to the table; be fed and united in the body and blood of Christ.

Post-Communion Blessing

P May the body and blood of Jesus Christ carry you in your vocation, and keep your heart filled with mercy.

C Amen.

Post-Communion Prayer

A Let us pray. Lord God,

C we give thanks that you have brought the good news to us once again in your body and blood. As we are joined in this meal once again with you, may we stretch the bounds of your family, bringing home all who are scattered. Amen.

Benediction

P *May God shield you in your trials, may Christ + strengthen you for each day, and may the Spirit light your path on your journey.*

C Amen.

Dismissal

A Go in peace, seek the lost, bring them home.

C Thanks be to God.

"Christ's Mass" is the festival set aside for the arrival of Jesus. It similarly refers to the twelve-day season, which begins on December 25 and concludes on January 5. We gather this day in awe at the Word made flesh and at God's passion for the creation.

For Christmas Eve, there are two services here. One is designed as a youth and family service and largely built around storytelling; the other is a more traditional liturgy with standard pieces in place. Each continues to build on the concept introduced in Advent of being on a journey to Christ. The star (if used during Advent) should be placed at the front of the nave near the cross if decoration and space allow.

The Sunday after Christmas (Christmas 1) has for its theme the concept of dwelling. As Christ has called us from all directions to himself, for a Sunday we learn what it is to exist, live, stay, and dwell with God.

If you have candles at your service, don't discard them. There is a proposal to bring them back at Pentecost.

Youth And Family Service

This service takes a good bit of preparation and explanation; the recommended liturgy will be laid out on the following pages. The main concept is that a fictional character named *Ferdinand* (meaning "journey") gets wind of something significant happening. He then begins the journey of discovery and along the way encounters the biblical characters. Depending on the multimedia capabilities of your setting, there are a number of ways to enhance the storytelling. The overall picture is that each story adds a bit of color to Ferdinand and at the end, he is fully colored in for his time with the Holy Family. There are recommendations in the liturgy for which colors to use and when.

At each bit of storytelling, there is a specific color of glowstick to be used; these must be passed out beforehand and most likely to the children of the congregation. This can either be used as a supplement or a replacement for candles on Christmas Eve; we first used it as a supplement, and it worked very well. Six different colored glowsticks are needed for the story and will need to be purchased beforehand. Each storytelling section begins with asking those who have a certain color glowstick to break it and shake it so that it begins to glow. As this is taking place, the storyteller takes a moment to say what each color symbolizes.

If you have the ability for projection, I recommend finding a picture of a young man from a coloring book or having someone draw one. Have your Sunday school, or any other children's group in the congregation, color a page with just the first color of the storytelling (they can either color one piece, like Ferdinand's hair, or color the whole thing in the one color). The next page should be colored with two colors (Ferdinand's hair and shirt, or the whole thing in two colors) and so on, until the last page is colored with all six colors. At each stage of storytelling, project the image with the appropriate colors.

For the candlelighting, have everyone with glowsticks raise them high in the air. It will create a beautiful mosaic in the congregation.

Traditional Service

This service assumes a context in which the Western Rite remains in place and is highlighted by the theme running through the Advent, Christmas, and Epiphany seasons. If you are in a setting where both types of services are being used, making a mural in Sunday school or other children's group to use on Christmas Eve is an excellent way to tie the two services together. Have the children color a large nativity set, placing it on black construction or butcher paper and taping twinkling Christmas lights on the back, shining through the black paper. The ground is made with green construction/butcher paper. A possible construction is provided below. The characters of the nativity can all be colored by the children, the star as well. The lights will need to be pressed through, so small holes will need to be cut. LED lights are best because they do not create heat against the paper.

Nativity Of Our Lord

Christmas Theme: Coming Home

Texts
Proper I
   Isaiah 9:2-7; Psalm 96; Titus 2:11-14; Luke 2:1-14 (15-20)
Proper II
   Isaiah 62:6-12; Psalm 97; Titus 3:4-7; Luke 2:(1-7) 8-20
Proper III
   Isaiah 52:7-10; Psalm 98; Hebrews 1:1-4 (5-12); John 1:1-14

Music Of The Day Traditional Hymns
"O Come, All Ye Faithful" (ELW283, UMH234, GG133, H83)
"Hark! The Herald Angels Sing" (ELW270, UMH240, GG119, H87)
"The First Noel" (ELW300, UMH245, GG147, H109)
"O Little Town Of Bethlehem" (ELW279, UMH230, GG121, H79)
"What Child Is This?" (ELW296, UMH219, GG145, H115)
"Silent Night" (ELW281, UMH239, GG134, H11)
"Joy To The World" (ELW267, UMH246, GG122, H100)

Music Of The Day Contemporized Christmas Carols
The following Christmas carols can be successfully sung by the congregation and played with contemporary praise band instrumentation from lead sheets found on ccli.com, such as drums, bass, guitars, keyboards.
"O Come, All Ye Faithful"
"Hark, The Herald Angels Sing"
"Angels We Have Heard On High"
"What Child Is This?"
"Silent Night"
"Joy To The World"

Music Of The Day Contemporary Songs
The following songs are geared for praise band without congregational singing.
"Born Is The King" (It's Christmas) by Crocker/Ligertwood (ccli.com SongSelect)
"Breath Of Heaven" by Eaton/Grant (ccli.com SongSelect)
"Christmas Canon Rock" by Trans-Siberian Orchestra (musicnotes.com)
"Christmas Eve Sarajevo" by Trans-Siberian Orchestra (musicnotes.com)
"Christmas Offering" by Paul Baloche (ccli.com SongSelect)
"Emmanuel" (Hallowed Manger Ground) by Tomlin/Cash (ccli.com SongSelect)
"Glory To God" by Reuben Morgan (ccli.com SongSelect)
"He Has Come For Us" (God Rest Ye Merry Gentlemen) by Ingram/Andrews (ccli.com SongSelect)

"I Heard The Bells On Christmas Day" by Hall/Oliver/Wasson (praisecharts.com)

"Joy To The World" (Unspeakable Joy) by Handel/Tomlin/Cash et al

"O Come Let Us Adore Him" by Wade/Crocker/Hardman/Taubert (ccli.com SongSelect)

"O Rejoice" by Mia Fieldes (ccli.com SongSelect)

"Sing Noel" by O'Brien/Carswell (ccli.com SongSelect)

"The First Noel" (Holy Is The Lord) by Hardman/Ligertwood/Wood (ccli.com SongSelect)

"Winter Snow" by Audrey Assad (praisecharts.com)

Invocation

P   Come, Father, and welcome us to your kingdom.

C   **Call us your children and give us your peace.**

P   Come, O Christ, and lighten our life.

C   **Shine into our darkness and bring us to light.**

P   Come, Holy Spirit, and waken our bones.

C   **Breathe joy and hope into our community.**

Apostolic Greeting

P   May the grace and love of God the Father, Son, and Holy Spirit welcome you home.

C   **Amen.**

Prayer Of The Day

P   Let us pray. God, on this night,

C   **the division between divine and human is destroyed. You offer us your very self in a child; humble, quiet, and yet you have disrupted the whole creation. Stir our hearts by the arrival of what we have begged for and sought since our very creation, your presence among us: Jesus Christ our Lord. Amen.**

Prayers Of The Church

A   The eyes of all look to you, O Lord. This day we ask, "How long?" for those who suffer. We lay before you this day the names and the challenges that weigh upon our hearts *(pause for silence)*. You bring hope to those despairing, and you bring peace to those unsettled. We pray this day that all may know you and your presence in this world. May Christmas be for each, not a day and celebration held once a year, but an orientation for how we engage one another. May we tend to the tasks granted to us with your guidance at our hands. Give our minds and hearts shelter and direction. For all that falls outside of our control, give us wisdom that we may trust you are there in good and ill, always and forever our Savior, Jesus Christ. Amen.

Offertory Prayer

P   Let us pray. God, Emmanuel,

C   **you have gifted us with your very self, more than we could ever hope. As we return what you have given to us, may it serve you and serve all of creation, so that the story of Jesus Christ be proclaimed far and near. Amen.**

Communion Welcome

P Come, Christ is welcoming you to the feast,

C Amen.

Post-Communion Prayer

A Let us pray. Lord God,

C in this bread and cup of Christ's very life, you give us food for our journey. As you led the magi by a star, as you brought the holy family home again, guide us on the way unfolding before us. Wherever we go, may our lives proclaim good news of great joy in Jesus Christ our Lord. Amen.

The Service Of Light

"Silent Night" is played quietly underneath dialogue as candles are lit and the light is passed. Once all candles are lit, the lights are dimmed, and the congregation sings all verses. The blessing concludes the ceremony, and the lights are turned back on when the congregation replies, "Merry Christmas!"

P The light shines in the darkness,

C and the darkness has not overcome it.

P The true light, which enlightens everyone,

C is coming into the world.

P You are the light of the world. Let your light shine before others that they may see your good works and glorify your Father in heaven.

C Amen.

Blessing

P May your eyes see, may your ears hear, may your hearts love, may your minds meditate, may your hands work, may your feet walk, and may your whole being follow the good news of Jesus Christ, the peace of the world.

C Amen.

P Merry Christmas!

C Merry Christmas!

Dismissal

P Go in peace! Love like no other!

C Thanks be to God!

Nativity Of Our Lord

Family Service
Christmas Theme: Coming Home

Texts
Proper I
       Isaiah 9:2-7; Psalm 96; Titus 2:11-14; Luke 2:1-14 (15-20)
Proper II
       Isaiah 62:6-12; Psalm 97; Titus 3:4-7; Luke 2:(1-7), 8-20
Proper III
       Isaiah 52:7-10; Psalm 98; Hebrews 1:1-4 (5-12); John 1:1-14

Theme Alternative Texts
*This service uses only the Luke 2:1-20 reading in its original form. The proposed liturgy follows all of the pieces of the Western Rite, but moves them around to blend with the pieces of the story. Each story could include an introduction to the biblical characters (excepting innkeeper since that character does not exist biblically) if it makes sense for the context; however, you may want to modify the Luke 2 reading if going this route. Recommendations would then be: **1) Herod:** Matthew 2:1-3, 7-8; **2) Wise Men:** Matthew 2:9-10; **3) Angels:** Luke 2:13-14; **4) Shepherds:** Luke 2:8-9, 15; **5) Innkeeper:** Luke 2:5-7; **6) Holy Family:** Luke 2: 16-20.*

Music Of The Day
The music suggestions for this Family Service are included in the order of service below. Traditional Christmas carols have been selected with familiarity and ease of singing for children in mind. It is essential that the children feel that they can actively participate in all parts of this service, including the singing. If you are working within time limits for your worship service, it is strongly suggested that you consider choosing a verse or two from some of the included carols, instead of singing the full songs.

Welcome
Here, the explanation of the glowsticks, storytelling, and liturgy belongs. Any other housekeeping or other announcements belong here as well. Ferdinand is an imagined character, who walks the route from his home to finding Jesus and along the way meets several of the characters from the biblical narrative and learns lessons from them. "Ferdinand" is a Spanish name meaning "Journey." Just as we have journeyed together from all over the world during the season of Advent, we now move together toward the manger and the Christ Child.

Carol – "O Come, All Ye Faithful" (ELW283, UMH234, GG133, H83)

The Story Of Ferdinand And King Herod
Red glowsticks are lit, symbolizing Power
This is our friend, Ferdinand. Ferdinand did not have many things to occupy his time. He just went from one day to the next, finding odd jobs to make enough money to keep warm and fed. He had no family nearby, but called the people he worked around "brother" and "sister." Ferdinand could disappear in an instant, and most people probably wouldn't notice. This idea didn't bother him, but it did make him wonder about those *really* important people in the world who everybody knew and loved.

One day, as he was cleaning out the horse stalls at a local farm, he started hearing a story that the king was nervous. Surely, anything making the king nervous was something worth looking into, so he asked his boss about this news. The farmer didn't know if he even believed the king was nervous, so he laughed and suggested that Ferdinand go ask the king himself. Not thinking for a moment that the farmer was joking, Ferdinand walked over and asked the guards if he could talk to King Herod about what was bothering him. King Herod was suspicious that Ferdinand knew something, so he invited him inside.

Quickly, Ferdinand asked King Herod how he could help, and the king realized that Ferdinand knew nothing, so he had better brush him off. King Herod told Ferdinand that there was some nonsense a few days ago about a baby king being born, and it all started because some wise men making a fuss around town. "If you ask me," said the king, "little things like babies are nothing special and certainly nothing worth getting excited about. I doubt if anyone will ever even be talking about this in two months. I'm not worried about it at all, but if you want to know more, those wise men went out of town that way; maybe you should go ask them." And Ferdinand thanked the king and started along the path to find the wise men.

Exchange of Peace

Carol – "We Three Kings Of Orient Are" (WOV646, UMH254, GG151, H128)

The Story Of Ferdinand And The Three Wisemen
Blue glowsticks are lit, symbolizing loyalty.
After traveling for a while, Ferdinand came upon the camp where the wise men had settled along the road. Ferdinand grew excited because this meant he was traveling the right way. He told the wise men about his trip to go see King Herod and how Herod sent him to find them to learn more. Ferdinand was excited to figure out why a small baby would be the type of thing that a king would talk about.

The wise men spoke of their studies, and how the world waited ages for this moment in time when someone of serious significance would be born. They themselves had always lived a blessed life, but the stars indicated that this newborn child would be something the world had never seen before. They set out with gifts of gold, and frankincense, and myrrh to give to this new baby king — as a thanks, but mostly as an offering of gifts from their own property. They spoke of the star that marked the direction of their travel, and Ferdinand looked up and saw what he thought they were referring to.

"But what's that other light over there?" asked Ferdinand. The wise men replied, "We're not sure, but it seems to be close to the place marked by the star. Maybe if you want to know more, that would be the place to go."

Ferdinand set out from the wise men and went to figure out why there was another light in the sky.

Carol – "Hark! The Herald Angels Sing" (ELW270, UMH240, GG119, H87)

The Story Of Ferdinand And The Angels

Yellow glowsticks are lit, symbolizing happiness.

The light grew brighter and brighter as Ferdinand approached. Eventually, it got so bright that he couldn't see where his next step was going to land. But he kept walking toward it, reaching his hands out in front to make sure he didn't run into anything. Suddenly, a voice came from the light, crying out, "Do not be afraid!" Which, of course, made Ferdinand afraid. He asked back, "Who are you?" "We are the angels of the Lord. We have come forward to make a very important announcement." "Does this have anything to do with a baby?" Ferdinand inquired. The angels replied, "Yes, have you heard?"

Ferdinand thought for a moment. He really didn't know too much, other than where he was supposed to go and that some important baby was there. He told the angels that he was excited to get there and find out. The angels told him of the shepherds who usually work on this hill who have an important story to tell, and they would have more details.

Ferdinand said, "All right, I will go and find them, but can you answer one quick question?" The angels agreed, and he asked them, "Why do you have to be so bright?" Making out a smile on one of the angel's faces, he heard her say, "Because there are so many things in the world that can distract your vision. The best way to grab and hold attention is to remove all the distractions and focus on the message." That sounded good enough for Ferdinand, and he focused on his task of going to find the shepherds.

Offering and Offering Carol – "The First Noel" (ELW300, UMH245, GG147, H109)

Offertory Prayer

P   Let us pray. Good and loving God,

C   **we rejoice in the birth of Jesus, who came among the poor to bring the riches of your grace. As you have blessed us with your gifts, let them be blessings for others. With the trees of the field, with all earth and heaven, we shout for joy at the coming of your Son, Jesus Christ our Lord. Amen.**

The Story Of Ferdinand And The Shepherds

Green glowsticks are lit, symbolizing growth and the grass that the sheep eat.

Ferdinand ran up to the shepherds, excited to have tracked them down so quickly. "Mr. Shepherds, Mr. Shepherds," he yelled. The shepherds were a little surprised at first, but it didn't take too long and they settled into a conversation with Ferdinand about the angels and their message. "We were just tending to our sheep," said the shepherds, "when from out of nowhere this light nearly blinded us and told us to not be afraid. Then there were all these songs being sung, and sheesh, it was all a bit overwhelming." Ferdinand told them about how he, too, had encountered the angels and was similarly shocked and amazed. But he wanted to know more.

"Did the angels tell you anything special?" he asked. They began to tell him all about how the angels told them that they would become some of the most important people of all time. "Are you going to be kings?" Ferdinand questioned. "No," the shepherds answered, "it was quite the opposite; we weren't going to become anything other than shepherds, but that we would be remembered always. What the angels taught us was that it wasn't necessarily about *what* we do, as if we needed to change jobs to be important, but about *how* we do the things we do and why we do them. Apparently, our whole lives will become changed by this one important event." Ferdinand just *had* to know what he was getting into. The shepherds told him, as he went running from their company, that the star was hovering over Bethlehem, and that he was nearly at the goal of this whole journey.

Gospel Welcome – "Go, Tell It On The Mountain" (ELW290, GG136, UMH251, H99, LBW70)

Gospel – Luke 2:1-20

The Story Of Ferdinand And The Innkeeper

Purple glowsticks are lit, symbolizing dignity.

Ferdinand ran as fast as he could to the building the star seemed to be shining upon. He went in to the front desk at the inn and found the innkeeper inside. "Sir!" he exclaimed. "Are you aware of what's going on here?" "Yeah, I'm swamped," replied the innkeeper, "because it's Christmastime. My rooms have been booked for months so I'm sorry, but you'll have to find some other place to stay." "But what about the baby?" cried Ferdinand. "Oh, I didn't realize you were with them," said the innkeeper. "Well, as I told you, there aren't any rooms; I've been sending people away for a few weeks now because of this census. I pride myself on a fine establishment here, but I can only do so much. These people just came in yesterday, and man, I could tell they were desperate. I felt awful, throwing them back out in the streets, so I cleared off a spot in the barn and threw a few blankets out there. Normally, I wouldn't think twice, but sometimes a surprise comes along, and it makes you really think about what's important; and you just have to do something about it. Go run around back. I think they're still awake."

Carol – "O Little Town Of Bethlehem" (ELW279, UMH230, GG121, H79)

Holy Communion

Communion Music – "Away In A Manger" (ELW277, UMH217, GG115, LBW67)

Post-Communion Prayer

P   Let us pray. God of wonder,

C   **in this bread and cup of Christ's very life, you give us food for our journey. As you led the magi by a star, as you brought the holy family home again, guide us on the way unfolding before us. Wherever we go, may our lives proclaim good news of great joy in Jesus Christ our Lord. Amen.**

The Story Of Ferdinand And The Holy Family

Pink glowsticks are lit, symbolizing love.

The scene was set. The father, the mother, and the newborn child all looked at each other lovingly. All of the sprinting and haste of the journey ground to a halt as Ferdinand beheld what was truly a special and holy moment. His mind raced through the events of the journey and the people whom he met along the way. He learned that this child would interrupt the everyday flow of life; this child would ask us to give all that we are; this baby will call for all of our attention and focus; this child would lead us to service in all of our vocations; this baby would teach us to look for surprises; and, the most importantly, this child would teach us to love like no other. Most importantly, this God will be among us and continue to love us like never before.

The Service Of Light – "Silent Night" (ELW281, UMH239, GG134, H11)

"Silent Night" is played quietly underneath dialogue as candles are lit and the light is passed. Once all candles are lit, the lights are dimmed, and the congregation sings all verses. The blessing concludes the ceremony, and the lights are turned back on when the congregation replies, "Merry Christmas!"

P The light shines in the darkness,
C **and the darkness has not overcome it.**
P The true light, which enlightens everyone,
C **is coming into the world.**
P You are the light of the world. Let your light shine before others that they may see your good works and glorify your Father in heaven....
C **Amen.**

Blessing

P May your eyes see, may your ears hear, may your hearts love, may your minds meditate, may your hands work, may your feet walk, and may your whole being follow the good news of Jesus Christ, the peace of the world.
C **Amen.**
P Merry Christmas!
C **Merry Christmas!**

Sending Carol – "Joy To The World" (ELW267, UMH246, GG122, H100)

Dismissal

P Go in peace! Love like no other!
C **Thanks be to God!**

Nativity Of Our Lord III

It would be a good idea to do a hymn-sing today, but a liturgy exists as well

Texts
Proper I
     Isaiah 9:2-7; Psalm 96; Titus 2:11-14; Luke 2:1-14 (15-20)
Proper II
     Isaiah 62:6-12; Psalm 97; Titus 3:4-7; Luke 2:(1-7), 8-20
Proper III
     Isaiah 52:7-10; Psalm 98; Hebrews 1:1-4 (5-12); John 1:1-14

Music Of The Day Traditional Hymns
"Angels We Have Heard On High" (ELW289, LBW71, GG113, UMH238, H96)
"Good Christian Friends, Rejoice" (ELW288, LBW55, GG132, UMH224, H107)
"Of The Father's Love Begotten" (ELW295, LBW42, GG108, UMH184, H82)
"Away In A Manger" (ELW277, GG115, UMH217)
"In The Bleak Midwinter" (ELW294, GG144, UMH221, H112)
"Silent Night" (ELW281, UMH239, GG134, H11)
"Joy To The World" (ELW267, UMH246, GG122, H100)

Music Of The Day Contemporized Christmas Carols
The following Christmas carols can be successfully sung by the congregation and played with contemporary praise band instrumentation from lead sheets found on ccli.com, such as drums, bass, guitars, keyboards.
"Angels We Have Heard On High"
"Go Tell It On The Mountain"
"Away In A Manger"
"Silent Night"
"Joy To The World"

Music Of The Day Contemporary Songs
"Born Is The King" (It's Christmas) by Crocker/Ligertwood (ccli.com SongSelect)
"When Love Was Born" by Schultz (ccli.com SongSelect)
"Emmanuel" by Alexander/Story (ccli.com SongSelect)
"Joy To The World" (Unspeakable Joy) by Watts/Handel/Tomlin et al (ccli.com SongSelect)

Important Items
     The festival for Saint Stephen is on December 26.

     The festival for Saint John is on December 27.

     The festival for the Holy Innocents is on December 28.

Invocation

P   We invite you, God of this place, Father, Son, and Holy Spirit to carry us as we pray and sing.

C   **Amen.**

Confession And Forgiveness

P   May we offer to God all of who we are, opening up to God's judgment and reconciliation.

P   God of all life,

C   **we seek to be returned as brothers and sisters of Christ. We have not served well as your chosen people, we have limited your grace, we have excluded parts of your creation, we have selfishly kept your gifts for ourselves. Call us again to your abundance and forgive us our sins, through our Savior, Jesus Christ.**

P   God has not abandoned his people. By his very presence, your sin is cast out. In the name of the Father, Son, and Holy Spirit, know your place at the Lord's table.

C   **Amen.**

Apostolic Greeting

P   Grace and peace to you; may we rejoice in God with all living things.

C   **Amen.**

Prayer Of The Day

A   Let us pray. God who shelters us,

C   **today we marvel at your Word made flesh. Into time and space you have come, not to control us, but to serve and love in the humblest form. Remember us in your mercy, and hold us in awe this day. Amen.**

Prayers Of The Church

A   Come, with voices united, let us plead to God on behalf of our brothers and sisters:

(after each petition, respond with)

A   As your children cry out,

C   **remember your mercy!**

(at the close of the prayers)

A   Remember, O Lord, and redeem those for whom we pray this day through the life of Jesus Christ our Savior.

C   **Amen.**

Offertory Prayer

A Let us pray. God of abundance,

C **we give thanks for your gifts, which you hand over to us to tend. As we return these gifts to you, may you receive them and bless them for the sake of your entire creation. In your holy name, we pray. Amen.**

Proper Preface

P It is indeed right, our duty and our joy, to offer praise with all of creation to you, Father and Lord of all. By your presence, you wash away the sins of all the saints and draw us once again to communion with you in your house forever, where we join together with the saints in their unending hymn. (Sanctus)

Communion Welcome

P Come, Christ is welcoming you to the feast.

Post-Communion Blessing

P May the body and blood of Jesus Christ, only begotten Son, keep you in his grace now and forever.

C **Amen.**

Post-Communion Prayer

A Let us pray. God of wonder,

C **in this bread and cup of Christ's very life, you give us food for our journey. As you led the magi by a star, as you brought the holy family home again, guide us on the way unfolding before us. Wherever we go, may our lives proclaim good news of great joy in Jesus Christ our Lord. Amen.**

Benediction

P May your eyes see, may your ears hear, may your hearts love, may your minds meditate, may your hands work, may your feet walk, and may your whole being follow the good news of Jesus Christ, the peace of the world.

C **Amen.**

P Merry Christmas!

C **Merry Christmas!**

Dismissal

A Go in peace! Love like no other!

C **Thanks be to God!**

Christmas 1

Texts
Isaiah 63:7-9
Psalm 148
Hebrews 2:10-18
Matthew 2:13-23

Music Of The Day Traditional Hymns
"O Come, All Ye Faithful" (ELW283, UMH234, GG133, H83)
"It Came Upon The Midnight Clear" (ELW282, GG123, UMH218, H89)
"That Boy-Child Of Mary" (ELW293, GG139, UMH241)
"The First Noel" (ELW300, UMH245, GG147, H109)
"What Child Is This?" (ELW296, UMH219, GG145, H115)
"Hark! The Herald Angels Sing" (ELW270, UMH240, GG119, H87)
"Silent Night" (ELW281, UMH239, GG134, H11)
"Joy To The World" (ELW267, UMH246, GG122, H100)

Music Of The Day Contemporized Christmas Carols
The following Christmas carols can be successfully sung by the congregation and played with contemporary praise band instrumentation from Lead Sheets found on ccli.com, such as Drums, Bass, Guitars, Keyboards.
"O Come, All Ye Faithful"
"Hark! the Herald Angels Sing"
"What Child Is This?"
"Silent Night"
"Joy To The World"

Music Of The Day Contemporary Songs
"Jesus, Name Above All Names" by Hearn (ccli.com SongSelect)
"Emmanuel" (Hallowed Manger Ground) by Tomlin/Cash (ccli.com SongSelect)
"He Has Come For Us" (God Rest Ye Merry Gentlemen) by Ingram/Andrews (ccli.com SongSelect)
"O Rejoice" by Mia Fieldes (ccli.com SongSelect)
"The First Noel" (Holy Is The Lord) by Hardman/Ligertwood/Wood (ccli.com SongSelect)

Important Items
The feast day for the Holy Name of Jesus is January 1. This day celebrates the circumcision and naming of Jesus from Luke 2:21.

It is also New Year's Day, making a prayer for renewal appropriate.

Invocation

P We invite you, God of this place, Father, Son, and Holy Spirit to carry us as we pray and sing.

C Amen.

Confession And Forgiveness

P May we offer to God all of who we are, opening up to God's judgment and reconciliation.

P God of all life,

C we seek to be returned as brothers and sisters of Christ. We have not served well as your chosen people, we have limited your grace, we have excluded parts of your creation, we have selfishly kept your gifts for ourselves. Call us again to your abundance and forgive us our sins, through our Savior, Jesus Christ.

P God has not abandoned his people. By his very presence, your sin is cast out. In the name of the Father, Son, and Holy Spirit, know your place at the Lord's table.

C Amen.

Apostolic Greeting

P Grace and peace to you; may we rejoice in God with all living things.

C Amen.

Prayer Of The Day

A Let us pray. God who shelters us,

C watch over our going out and coming in. Remember us, according to your covenant. Shield us from the evils of this world, and keep us always seeking your mercy — so that we may share that good news with all who need to hear. We pray through your Son, Jesus Christ our Lord. Amen.

Prayers Of The Church

A Come, with voices united, let us plead to God on behalf of our brothers and sisters:

(after each petition, respond with)

A As your children cry out,

C remember your mercy!

(at the close of the prayers)

A Remember, O Lord, and redeem those for whom we pray this day through the life of Jesus Christ our Savior.

C Amen.

Offertory Prayer

A Let us pray. God of abundance,

C we give thanks for your gifts that you hand over to us to tend. As we return these gifts to you, may

you receive them and bless them for the sake of your entire creation. **In your holy name, we pray. Amen.**

Proper Preface

P   It is indeed right, our duty and our joy, to offer praise with all of creation to you, Father and Lord of all. By your presence, you wash away the sins of all the saints and draw us once again to communion with you in your house forever, where we join together with the saints in their unending hymn. (Sanctus)

Communion Welcome

P   Come, Christ is welcoming you to the feast.

Post-Communion Blessing

P   May the body and blood of Jesus Christ, only begotten Son, keep you in his grace now and forever.
C   **Amen.**

Post-Communion Prayer

A   Let us pray. God of wonder,
C   **in this bread and cup of Christ's very life, you give us food for our journey. As you led the magi by a star, as you brought the holy family home again, guide us on the way unfolding before us. Wherever we go, may our lives proclaim good news of great joy in Jesus Christ our Lord. Amen.**

Benediction

P   May your eyes see, may your ears hear, may your hearts love, may your minds meditate, may your hands work, may your feet walk, and may your whole being follow the good news of Jesus Christ, the peace of the world.
C   **Amen.**
P   Merry Christmas!
C   **Merry Christmas!**

Dismissal

A   Go in peace! Love like no other!
C   **Thanks be to God!**

Season Of Epiphany

Epiphany is the time when God is "revealed" to us. There are several definitions for the word — a direct transliteration of the Greek — like manifestation, an awareness, and so on. For the sake of this season in particular, the themes built in Advent and Christmas continue to play out. Christ will be revealed as our center, or home, and Epiphany will be a time when we discover how we know that Christ is those things, as well as how we act when we acknowledge that reality.

There is an option to celebrate Epiphany on a Sunday, which would use the readings for the festival day. Alternatively, you could celebrate the Baptism Of Our Lord on either the First Sunday after the Epiphany, or the Second Sunday after the Epiphany, or omit it altogether. Without question, the more water you use on the festival of the Baptism Of Our Lord the better. Grab an aspergillum or a palm branch, and remind people of their baptism by letting them get wet in church. Also, if you have a large font, hold a special time with the children of the congregation at the baptismal font, and let them stir the water with their hands. If possible, try to schedule a baptism for that day.

The star used during Christmas and Advent should be present through the end of Epiphany. The star, as designed, is the Epiphany star.

As the arrival of the wise men marks the beginning of the season, there is an option to incorporate that image as part of the worship for the Season of Epiphany. In most mainline traditions, offering is given via a plate passed from one worshiper to the next. During this season, it is proposed that for offering, you invite people to bring forward their offering to the altar themselves, rather than leaving that task for the ushers. There should still be some sort of offering music, though the specific offertory hymn, which is usually played and sung while the gifts are brought forward, should be omitted. If using this method, make sure to introduce the offering with language that invites people to bring their gifts forward and ties the act in worship to the story of the wise men. While this will undoubtedly bring anxiety to some, especially those who are unable to give at the time, it should coincide with people writing notes of thanks to God. Invite people to put both in the envelopes (or just one) and to come forward as families to offer their gifts of both money and thanks to God in worship. The thanks from the week before should be included in the prayers of the church the following week.

Possible introduction:
P   Let us bring our gifts and our thanks forward to God with our offering.

Epiphany Of Our Lord

Texts
Isaiah 60:1-6
Psalm 72:1-7, 10-14
Ephesians 3:1-12
Matthew 2:1-12

Music Of The Day Traditional Hymns
"We Three Kings Of Orient Are" (WOV646, UMH254, GG151, H128)
"Arise, Your Light Is Come" (ELW314, GG744)
"Beautiful Savior/Fairest Lord Jesus" (ELW838, GG630, H384)
"Shine, Jesus, Shine" (ELW671, GG192, WOV651)
"Brightest And Best Of The Stars" (ELW303, H117)

Music Of The Day Contemporary Songs
"Here I Am To Worship" by Tim Hughes (ccli.com SongSelect)
"Light Of The World" by Redman (ccli.com SongSelect)
"All The Heavens" by Avery/Carr/Powell/Anderson (ccli.com SongSelect)
"Father Of Lights" by John Barnett (ccli.com SongSelect)
"Shine, Jesus, Shine" by Kendrick (ccli.com SongSelect)

Invocation
P   Bring your dawn to us, + Father, Son, and Holy Spirit, and send your glory upon us.
C   **Amen.**

Confession And Forgiveness
P   Let us call upon the Lord, seeking to be joined together once again.
(pause for reflection)
P   God, most righteous,
C   **we have been worried about all manner of wrong things. We have put priority on treasures we can hold. We have trusted in our own abilities and pushed you to the side. Reveal yourself again to us that we may be free from our burdens and return to you. Amen.**
P   God's grace comes to Jew, Gentile, and all. Through the promise in Jesus Christ, your sins are taken away. Rejoice! For yours are the blessings of the Almighty.
C   **Amen.**

Apostolic Greeting

P The God who reveals himself in Christ, grant you grace and may his love be with you always.

C **And also with you.**

Prayer Of The Day

A Let us pray. Lord Jesus,

C **to all who know you, you reveal yourself as light and life. As the wise men gathered at your side and bowed in worship, so shape and guide our understanding. Teach us to pray, teach us to shine, teach us to love, through Jesus Christ our Lord. Amen.**

Prayers Of The Church

A Your children wander without you, God. Draw near to us as we call out to you

(Pause for reflection)

(After each petition)

A To you, we pray;

C **send us your blessings.**

(After the last petition)

A For each joy and pain we bring to you, and for all the needs and celebrations in the world, reveal yourself to us as life-giver, through Jesus Christ our Lord.

C **Amen.**

Offertory Prayer

A Let us pray. God of all things,

C **we offer to you these gifts, for which we give thanks. As you have blessed us by them, we return them to you, so that they may be a blessing to the ends of the earth. Use them for the creation and all its needs, through Jesus Christ our Lord. Amen.**

Proper Preface

P It is right, our duty and our joy, that we should in all that we do give thanks and praise to you, our light, our life, and our home. As you reveal your passion to us through Jesus Christ, we marvel at how your faithfulness abounds. We respond with gladness that our creator would dwell so closely with us. Let us join with our brothers and sisters of all times and places in the unending hymn:

Communion Welcome

P Come and eat; Christ has been poured out for you.

Post-Communion Blessing

P May the Word made flesh give you new life to proclaim the good news always.

C **Amen.**

Post-Communion Prayer

A Let us pray. Emmanuel,

C **with this bread and wine, you have once again shown us how you welcome even the least of all the saints to a place near you. Help us to be driven by your gifts to go forth in boldness and confidence to share faith and declare to the world who you truly are, our merciful Savior and Lord. Amen.**

Benediction

P May God our Father shield you, may + Christ lift your burdens, and the Holy Spirit give life to your steps.

C **Amen.**

Dismissal

P Go forward to proclaim Jesus Christ!

C **For the sake of the good news! Amen!**

Baptism Of Our Lord

Texts
Isaiah 42:1-9
Psalm 29
Acts 10:34-43
Matthew 3:13-17

Music Of The Day Traditional Hymns
"Baptized In Water" (ELW456, GG482)
"Wade In The Water" (ELW459)
"I Was There To Hear Your Borning Cry" (ELW732, GG488)
"Shine, Jesus, Shine" (ELW671, GG192, WOV651)
"Go, My Children, With My Blessing" (ELW543, GG547)

Music Of The Day Contemporary Songs
"The River Is Here" by Andy Park (ccli.com SongSelect)
"Famous One" by Tomlin/Reeves (ccli.com SongSelect)
"Shine On Us" by Smith/Smith (ccli.com SongSelect)
"Shine On" by Bryson et al. (ccli.com SongSelect)
"Light Of The World" by Redman (ccli.com SongSelect)
"Father Of Lights" by John Barnett (ccli.com SongSelect)

Invocation *(gather at the baptismal font for the opening of the service)*
P   Blessed be our God and Father and our Lord Jesus Christ for carrying us when we fall.
C   Amen.

(The Confession And Forgiveness are replaced by a Remembrance Of Baptism for this day)

Remembrance Of Baptism *(Use a palm/aspergillum to sprinkle water upon congregation)*
P   In the waters of the great chaos, we find our roots. We remember the ways our God has delivered us through torment and into the promised land of new life.
C   Alleluia, thanks be to God!
P   When the storm covered the face of the earth, at the voice of God the waters were calmed and the earth came forward. Waters were separated from waters, and God created.
C   Alleluia, thanks be to God!
P   The storm rose again, flooding evil and washing it from the face of the earth. The rains came, and God cleansed.

C **Alleluia, thanks be to God!**

P Moses was saved by hiding in the water, and when Israel escaped its dreaded fate as slaves, Moses stood at the water and God opened the path to escape. The waters parted, and God saved.

C **Alleluia, thanks be to God!**

P In the river Jordan, Jesus entered and was baptized by John. In this water, we too are called children of God. The waters were poured, and God claimed.

C **Alleluia, thanks be to God!**

P May the waters of new life wash over us and remind us each day of your claim on each of us, and how you use water to create, cleanse, save, and claim each who calls out to you.

C **Amen!**

Apostolic Greeting

P The very Word of God grant you grace and peace this day.

C **Amen.**

Prayer Of The Day

A Let us pray. Christ, our brother,

C **we long for the day when we know you as well as you know us. By the water which gives us life, help us to trust that you are alive in us, and that we are renewed to be a light to the world, through Jesus Christ our Savior and Lord. Amen.**

Prayers Of The Church

A Washed and renewed as members of the body of Christ, let us approach God on behalf of those who need it.

(Silence for reflection)

A By your mercy,

C **hear our prayer.**

(After the last petition)

A Pour your Holy Spirit into each of us, that we may answer prayers on your behalf. Grant peace to all those who seek it through Jesus Christ.

C **Amen.**

Offertory Prayer

A Let us pray. Life-giving God,

C **all we have comes from you. All we are comes from you. All we give back comes from you. Take these gifts, bless and multiply them, so that the world may know of your faithfulness. Through Jesus Christ our Lord. Amen.**

Proper Preface

P It is indeed right that we should give thanks and praise to God for the waters that birthed us, cleanse us, and sustain us are testament to God still alive, giving us what we need for each day. As water cycles through its stages, we give thanks for how you have called this church in this time and this place, and together we raise one small voice to join with the great church of all times and places in this unending hymn. (Sanctus)

Communion Welcome
P   Christ has called you, brothers and sisters. Approach the table as one of the family.

Post-Communion Blessing
P   Now, may the body and blood of Jesus Christ continue to renew you for your baptismal calling this day and always.

C   **Amen.**

Post-Communion Prayer
A   Let us pray. Life-giving God,

C   **your mercy knows no ends. Teach us through the sacraments of baptism and Communion of the abundance of the gifts and promises you pour out. Strengthen us to pass along these blessings to those who beg for them. Amen.**

Benediction
P   You have been claimed by the Father, + Son, and Holy Spirit. May you take in the presence of God each time water touches your skin.

C   **Amen.**

Dismissal
A   Go in peace, called out to serve our neighbors.

C   **Amen!**

Texts
Isaiah 49:1-7
Psalm 40:1-11
1 Corinthians 1:1-9
John 1:29-42

Music Of The Day Traditional Hymns
"Here In This Place (Gather Us In)" (ELW532, WOV718, GG401)
"Here I Am, Lord/I, The Lord Of Sea And Sky" (ELW574, GG69, UMH593)
"Jesus Shall Reign" (ELW434, GG265, UMH157, H544, LBW530)
"Shine, Jesus, Shine" (ELW671, GG192, WOV651)
"Songs Of Thankfulness And Praise" (ELW310, H135)

Music Of The Day Contemporary Songs
"Forever" by Tomlin (ccli.com SongSelect)
"Dwell In Your House" by Ewing (ccli.com SongSelect)
"In The Light" by DCTalk (musicnotes.com)
"Shine" by Collective Soul *(Acoustic part of song only)* (musicnotes.com)
"Light Of The World" by Redman (ccli.com SongSelect)
"Father Of Lights" by John Barnett (ccli.com SongSelect)

Important Items
If your context has a particular history, Martin Luther King Jr.'s celebration is the third Monday in January.

The Week of Prayer for Christian Unity falls during the third week of January. A particular petition is included in this plan during the prayers of the church.

The feast day for the Confession of Saint Peter is on January 18.

Invocation
P   Bring your dawn to us, + Father, Son, and Holy Spirit, and send your glory upon us.
C   **Amen.**

Confession And Forgiveness
P   Let us call upon the Lord, seeking to be joined together once again.

(pause for reflection)

P   God, most righteous,

C   **we have been worried about all manner of wrong things. We have put priority on treasures we can hold. We have trusted in our own abilities and pushed you to the side. Reveal yourself again to us that we may be free from our burdens and return to you. Amen.**

P   God's grace comes to Jew, Gentile, and all. Through the promise in Jesus Christ, your sins are taken away. Rejoice! For yours are the blessings of the Almighty.

C   **Amen.**

Apostolic Greeting

P   The God who reveals himself in Christ, grant you grace, and may his love be with you always.

C   **And also with you.**

Prayer Of The Day

A   Let us pray. Lamb of God,

C   **you have called us from the beginning to be servants of the Word. Guide our hearts to be able to see all the ways you provide for this world, and teach our tongues to testify that you are Messiah, God's anointed for the sake of saving the world. Amen.**

Prayers Of The Church

A   Your children wander without you, God. Draw near to us as we call out to you.

(Pause for reflection)

(For the Week of Prayer for Christian Unity)

A   You have formed us in the womb to be one body, yet we have split and divided as if we have no need of one another. Stitch us back together, reminding us that none of us is the whole body, but that each piece of your church is in need of each other piece. For all our brothers and sisters, both close to us and distant, we long for the day when we all sing together again.

(After each petition)

A   To you, we pray.

C   **Send us your blessings.**

(After the last petition)

A   For each joy and pain we bring to you, and for all the needs and celebrations in the world, reveal yourself to us as life-giver, through Jesus Christ our Lord.

C   **Amen.**

Offertory Prayer

A   Let us pray. God of all things,

C   **we offer to you these gifts, for which we give thanks. As you have blessed us by them, we return them to you, so that they may be a blessing to the ends of the earth. Use them for the creation and all its needs, through Jesus Christ our Lord. Amen.**

Proper Preface

P   It is right, our duty and our joy, that we should in all that we do give thanks and praise to you, our light, our life, and our home. As you reveal your passion to us through Jesus Christ, we marvel at how your faithfulness abounds. We respond with gladness that our Creator would dwell so closely with us. Let us join with our brothers and sisters of all times and places in the unending hymn:

Communion Welcome

P   Come and eat; Christ has been poured out for you.

Post-Communion Blessing

P   May the Word made flesh give you new life to proclaim the good news always.
C   **Amen.**

Post-Communion Prayer

A   Let us pray. Emmanuel,
C   **with this bread and wine, you have once again shown us how you welcome even the least of all the saints to a place near you. Help us to be driven by your gifts to go forth in boldness and confidence to share faith and declare to the world who you truly are, our merciful Savior and Lord. Amen.**

Benediction

P   May God our Father shield you, may + Christ lift your burdens, and the Holy Spirit give life to your steps.
C   **Amen.**

Dismissal

P   Go forward to proclaim Jesus Christ!
C   **For the sake of the good news! Amen!**

Texts
Isaiah 9:1-4
Psalm 27:1, 4-9
1 Corinthians 1:10-18
Matthew 4:12-23

Music Of The Day Traditional Hymns

"Praise The Lord, O Heavens" (ELW823, H373)
"Will You Come And Follow Me" (ELW798, GG726)
"I Want To Walk As A Child Of The Light" (WOV649, GG377, UMH206, H490)
"The Spirit Sends Us Forth To Serve" (WOV723)
"We Are Marching In The Light" (WOV650, GG853)
"I Love To Tell The Story" (ELW661, GG462, UMH156)

Music Of The Day Contemporary Songs

"All Over The World" by Redman/Smith (ccli.com SongSelect)
"I Will Follow" by Tomlin (ccli.com SongSelect)
"Shine" by Salvador (musicnotes.com)
"It Is You" by Zschech (ccli.com SongSelect)
"Joyous Light" by Tomlin/Crowder (ccli.com SongSelect)
"Father Of Lights" by John Barnett (ccli.com SongSelect)

Important Items

The Week of Prayer for Christian Unity falls in the third week of January. A particular petition is included in this plan during the prayers of the church.

Invocation

P Bring your dawn to us, + Father, Son, and Holy Spirit, and send your glory upon us.
C Amen.

Confession And Forgiveness

P Let us call upon the Lord, seeking to be joined together once again.
(pause for reflection)
P God, most righteous,

C we have been worried about all manner of wrong things. We have put priority on treasures we can hold. We have trusted in our own abilities and pushed you to the side. Reveal yourself again to us that we may be free from our burdens and return to you. Amen.

P God's grace comes to Jew, to Gentile, and to all. Through the promise in Jesus Christ, your sins are taken away. Rejoice! For yours are the blessings of the Almighty.

C Amen.

Apostolic Greeting

P The God who reveals himself in Christ, grant you grace, and may his love be with you always.

C And also with you.

Prayer Of The Day

A Let us pray. Rabbi,

C you have brought us wisdom and light. Help us now to continue to follow, continue to seek, continue to long for you. Show us the ways that we still need repentance and call us, no matter how scary or challenging, to be servants of the gospel; in your holy name we pray. Amen.

Prayers Of The Church

A Your children wander without you, God. Draw near to us as we call out to you.
(Pause for reflection.)

(For the Week of Prayer for Christian Unity)

A You have formed us in the womb to be one body, yet we have split and divided as if we have no need of one another. Stitch us back together, reminding us that none of us is the whole body, but that each piece of your church is in need of each other piece. For all our brothers and sisters, both close to us and distant, we long for the day when we all sing together again.

(After each petition)

A To you, we pray.

C Send us your blessings.

(After the last petition)

A For each joy and pain we bring to you, and for all the needs and celebrations in the world, reveal yourself to us as life-giver, through Jesus Christ our Lord.

C Amen.

Offertory Prayer

A Let us pray. God of all things,

C we offer to you these gifts, for which we give thanks. As you have blessed us by them, we return them to you, so that they may be a blessing to the ends of the earth. Use them for the creation and all its needs, through Jesus Christ, our Lord. Amen.

Proper Preface

P It is right, our duty and our joy, that we should in all that we do give thanks and praise to you, our light, our life, and our home. As you reveal your passion to us through Jesus Christ, we marvel at how your faithfulness abounds. We respond with gladness that our Creator would dwell so closely with us. And now we join with our brothers and sisters of all times and places in the unending hymn:

Communion Welcome

P Come and eat; Christ has been poured out for you.

Post-Communion Blessing

P May the Word made flesh give you new life to proclaim the good news always.

C **Amen.**

Post-Communion Prayer

A Let us pray. Emmanuel,

C **with this bread and wine, you have once again shown us how you welcome even the least of all the saints to a place near you. Help us to be driven by your gifts to go forth in boldness and confidence to share faith and declare to the world who you truly are, our merciful Savior and Lord. Amen.**

Benediction

P May God our Father shield you, may + Christ lift your burdens, and the Holy Spirit give life to your steps.

C **Amen.**

Dismissal

P Go forward to proclaim Jesus Christ!

C **For the sake of the good news! Amen!**

Texts
Micah 6:1-8
Psalm 15
1 Corinthians 1:18-31
Matthew 5:1-12

Music Of The Day Traditional Hymns
"Blest Are They" (ELW728, GG172)
"Lord, Whose Love In Humble Service" (ELW712)
"Be Thou My Vision" (ELW793, GG450, UMH451, H488)
"God Of Grace And God Of Glory" (ELW705, GG307, UMH577, H594)
"We Are Called" (ELW720)
"God, Whose Almighty Word" (ELW673)

Music Of The Day Contemporary Songs
"Holy" by Brown (ccli.com SongSelect)
"Blessed" by Zschech/Morgan (ccli.com SongSelect)
"Endless Light" by Ussher/Cashwell (ccli.com SongSelect)
"Shine" by Salvador (musicnotes.com)
"It Is You" by Zschech (ccli.com SongSelect)
"Joyous Light" by Tomlin/Crowder (ccli.com SongSelect)

Important Items
The feast day for the Presentation of Our Lord is on February 2.

It may not seem all that significant, but Groundhog Day is celebrated on February 2. While it may seem hard to make a Christological point, nonetheless it's an example of how people gather around to see how light hits and bounces off an object.

Ash Wednesday is approaching. It may be a good time to start mentioning this and other Lenten plans.

Invocation
P   Bring your dawn to us, + Father, Son, and Holy Spirit, and send your glory upon us.
C   Amen.

Confession And Forgiveness

P   Let us call upon the Lord, seeking to be joined together once again.

(pause for reflection)

P   God, most righteous,

C   **we have been worried about all manner of wrong things. We have put priority on treasures we can hold. We have trusted in our own abilities and pushed you to the side. Reveal yourself again to us that we may be free from our burdens and return to you. Amen.**

P   God's grace comes to Jew, Gentile, and all. Through the promise in Jesus Christ, your sins are taken away. Rejoice! For yours are the blessings of the Almighty.

C   **Amen.**

Apostolic Greeting

P   The God who reveals himself in Christ, grant you grace, and may his love be with you always.

C   **And also with you.**

Prayer Of The Day

A   Let us pray. Christ, our teacher,

C   **train us how to see the world as you see it, not as we see each other. Help us not to be too proud or too ashamed to speak your truth of humility and love to a humanity that lacks a significant amount of both. This we pray through your holy name. Amen.**

Prayers Of The Church

A   Your children wander without you, God. Draw near to us as we call out to you.

(Pause for reflection)

(After each petition)

A   To you, we pray.

C   **Send us your blessings.**

(After the last petition)

A   For each joy and pain we bring to you, and for all the needs and celebrations in the world, reveal yourself to us as life-giver, through Jesus Christ our Lord.

C   **Amen.**

Offertory Prayer

A   Let us pray. God of all things,

C   **we offer to you these gifts, for which we give thanks. As you have blessed us by them, we return them to you, so that they may be a blessing to the ends of the earth. Use them for the creation and all its needs, through Jesus Christ our Lord. Amen.**

Proper Preface

P   It is right, our duty and our joy, that we should in all that we do give thanks and praise to you, our light, our life, and our home. As you reveal your passion to us through Jesus Christ, we marvel at how your faithfulness abounds. We respond with gladness that our Creator would dwell so closely with us. And now we join with our brothers and sisters of all times and places in the unending hymn. (Sanctus)

Communion Welcome

P   Come and eat; Christ has been poured out for you.

Post-Communion Blessing

P   May the Word made flesh give you new life to proclaim the good news always.
C   **Amen.**

Post-Communion Prayer

A   Let us pray. Emmanuel,
C   **with this bread and wine, you have once again shown us how you welcome even the least of all the saints to a place near you. Help us to be driven by your gifts to go forth in boldness and confidence to share faith and declare to the world who you truly are, our merciful Savior and Lord. Amen.**

Benediction

P   May God our Father shield you, may + Christ lift your burdens, and the Holy Spirit give life to your steps.
C   **Amen.**

Dismissal

P   Go forward to proclaim Jesus Christ!
C   **For the sake of the good news! Amen!**

Epiphany 5

Texts
Isaiah 58:1-9a (9b-12)
Psalm 112:1-9 (10)
1 Corinthians 2:1-12 (13-16)
Matthew 5:13-20

Music Of The Day Traditional Hymns
"This Little Light Of Mine" (ELW677, UMH585)
"Thy Holy Wings" (ELW613, UMH502)
"Christ, Be Our Light" (ELW715, GG314)
"Love Divine, All Loves Excelling" (ELW631, GG366, UMH384b, H657)
"O, For A Thousand Tongues To Sing" (ELW886, GG610, UMH57, H493)

Music Of The Day Contemporary Songs
"Salt And Light" by Engle (ccli.com SongSelect)
"We Are" by Jobe (ccli.com SongSelect)
"Endless Light" by Ussher/Cashwell (ccli.com SongSelect)
"Shine On Us" by Smith/Smith (ccli.com SongSelect)
"It Is You" by Zschech (ccli.com SongSelect)

Invocation
P   Bring your dawn to us, + Father, Son, and Holy Spirit, and send your glory upon us.
C   Amen.

Confession And Forgiveness
P   Let us call upon the Lord, seeking to be joined together once again.
(Pause for reflection)
P   God, most righteous,
C   we have been worried about all manner of wrong things. We have put priority on treasures we can hold. We have trusted in our own abilities and pushed you to the side. Reveal yourself again to us that we may be free from our burdens and return to you. Amen.
P   God's grace comes to Jew, Gentile, and all. Through the promise in Jesus Christ, your sins are taken away. Rejoice! For yours are the blessings of the Almighty.
C   Amen.

Apostolic Greeting

P The God who reveals himself in Christ, grant you grace, and may his love be with you always.

C **And also with you.**

Prayer Of The Day

A Let us pray. Ever-present God,

C **help us to live every day in you. Teach us that all you have given to us is meant to be used and shared each day of the week and not just when it suits us and only in the confines of worship. Be the hope of the world through us. We pray in the name of your Son, Jesus Christ. Amen.**

Prayers Of The Church

A Your children wander without you, God. Draw near to us as we call out to you.

(Pause for reflection)

(After each petition)

A To you, we pray.

C **Send us your blessings.**

(After the last petition)

A For each joy and pain we bring to you, and for all the needs and celebrations in the world, reveal yourself to us as life-giver, through Jesus Christ our Lord.

C **Amen.**

Offertory Prayer

A Let us pray. God of all things,

C **we offer to you these gifts, for which we give thanks. As you have blessed us by them, we return them to you, so that they may be a blessing to the ends of the earth. Use them for the creation and all its needs, through Jesus Christ our Lord. Amen.**

Proper Preface

P It is right, our duty and our joy, that we should in all that we do give thanks and praise to you, our light, our life, and our home. As you reveal your passion to us through Jesus Christ, we marvel at how your faithfulness abounds. We respond with gladness that our Creator would dwell so closely with us. And now we join with our brothers and sisters of all times and places in the unending hymn. (Sanctus)

Communion Welcome

P Come and eat; Christ has been poured out for you.

Post-Communion Blessing

P May the Word made flesh give you new life to proclaim the good news always.

C **Amen.**

Post-Communion Prayer

A Let us pray. Emmanuel,

C **with this bread and wine, you have once again shown us how you welcome even the least of all the saints to a place near you. Help us to be driven by your gifts to go forth in boldness and confidence to share faith and declare to the world who you truly are, our merciful Savior and Lord. Amen.**

Benediction

P May God our Father shield you, may + Christ lift your burdens, and the Holy Spirit give life to your steps.

C **Amen.**

Dismissal

P Go forward to proclaim Jesus Christ!

C **For the sake of the good news! Amen!**

Epiphany 6

Texts
Deuteronomy 30:15-20 alt (Sirach 15:15-20)
Psalm 119:1-8
1 Corinthians 3:1-9
Matthew 5:21-37

Music Of The Day Traditional Hymns
"Joyful, Joyful, We Adore Thee" (ELW836, LBW551, GG611, UMH89, H376)
"Lord God, We Praise You/Father, We Praise Thee" (ELW558, UMH680, H1)
"Day By Day" (ELW790)
"Healer Of Our Every Ill" (ELW612)
"O Master, Let Me Walk With You" (ELW818, GG738, UMH430, H660)

Music Of The Day Contemporary Songs
"This Is Amazing Grace" by Wickham (ccli.com SongSelect)
"Indescribable" by Story (ccli.com SongSelect)
"Forever Reign" by Morgan/Ingram (ccli.com SongSelect)
"Let The Peace Of God Reign" by Zschech (ccli.com SongSelect)
"Communion" by Powell/Avery et al (ccli.com SongSelect)

Important Items
If it is relevant to your context, Lincoln's birthday is February 12.

If it is relevant to your context, Valentine's Day is February 14.

Invocation
P   Bring your dawn to us, + Father, Son, and Holy Spirit, and send your glory upon us.
C   **Amen.**

Confession And Forgiveness
P   Let us call upon the Lord, seeking to be joined together once again.
(Pause for reflection)
P   God, most righteous,
C   **we have been worried about all manner of wrong things. We have put priority on treasures we can hold. We have trusted in our own abilities and pushed you to the side. Reveal yourself again to us that we may be free from our burdens and return to you. Amen.**

P God's grace comes to Jew, Gentile, and all. Through the promise in Jesus Christ, your sins are taken away. Rejoice! For yours are the blessings of the Almighty.

C **Amen.**

Apostolic Greeting

P The God who reveals himself in Christ, grant you grace, and may his love be with you always.

C **And also with you.**

Prayer Of The Day

A Let us pray. Christ, our judge,

C **you give to us the power to reason and choose. Help us to guard our minds to make the right choices. Yet, when we fail, give us the insight to return to you and trust in your mercy. We pray in your holy name. Amen.**

Prayers Of The Church

A Your children wander without you, God. Draw near to us as we call out to you.

(Pause for reflection)

(After each petition)

A To you, we pray.

C **Send us your blessings.**

(After the last petition)

A For each joy and pain we bring to you, and for all the needs and celebrations in the world, reveal yourself to us as life-giver, through Jesus Christ our Lord.

C **Amen.**

Offertory Prayer

A Let us pray. God of all things,

C **we offer to you these gifts, for which we give thanks. As you have blessed us by them, we return them to you, so that they may be a blessing to the ends of the earth. Use them for the creation and all its needs, through Jesus Christ our Lord. Amen.**

Proper Preface

P It is right, our duty and our joy, that we should in all that we do give thanks and praise to you, our light, our life, and our home. As you reveal your passion to us through Jesus Christ, we marvel at how your faithfulness abounds. We respond with gladness that our Creator would dwell so closely with us. And now we join with our brothers and sisters of all times and places in the unending hymn. (Sanctus)

Communion Welcome

P Come and eat; Christ has been poured out for you.

Post-Communion Blessing

P May the Word made flesh give you new life to proclaim the good news always.

C **Amen.**

Post-Communion Prayer

A Let us pray. Emmanuel,

C **with this bread and wine, you have once again shown us how you welcome even the least of all the saints to a place near you. Help us to be driven by your gifts to go forth in boldness and confidence to share faith and declare to the world who you truly are, our merciful Savior and Lord. Amen.**

Benediction

P May God our Father shield you, may + Christ lift your burdens, and the Holy Spirit give life to your steps.

C **Amen.**

Dismissal

P Go forward to proclaim Jesus Christ!

C **For the sake of the good news! Amen!**

Texts
Leviticus 19:1-2, 9-18
Psalm 119:33-40
1 Corinthians 3:10-11, 16-23
Matthew 5:38-48

Music Of The Day Traditional Hymns
"The Church's One Foundation" (ELW654, GG321, UMH545, H525)
"O Jesus, Joy Of Loving Hearts" (ELW658)
"Blest Be The Tie That Binds" (ELW656, GG306, UMH557)
"Built On A Rock" (ELW652)
"Jesus Shall Reign" (ELW434, GG265, UMH157, H544)
"Jesus Loves Me" (ELW595, GG188, UMH191)

Music Of The Day Contemporary Songs
"Today Is The Day" by Brewster/Baloche (ccli.com SongSelect)
"Because Of Your Love" by Baloche/Brown (ccli.com SongSelect)
"Made New" by Meeker/Brewster/Wedgeworth (ccli.com SongSelect)
"Love" by Pierce/Tomlin et al. (ccli.com SongSelect)
"Shout To The Lord" by Zschech (ccli.com SongSelect)
"Communion" by Powell/Avery et al (ccli.com SongSelect)

Important Items
If it is relevant to your context, Presidents Day and Washington's birthday are on February 20.

Invocation
P   Bring your dawn to us, + Father, Son, and Holy Spirit, and send your glory upon us.
C   Amen.

Confession And Forgiveness
P   Let us call upon the Lord, seeking to be joined together once again.
(Pause for reflection)
P   God, most righteous,
C   we have been worried about all manner of wrong things. We have put priority on treasures we can hold. We have trusted in our own abilities and pushed you to the side. Reveal yourself again to us that we may be free from our burdens and return to you. Amen.

P God's grace comes to Jew, Gentile, and all. Through the promise in Jesus Christ, your sins are taken away. Rejoice! For yours are the blessings of the Almighty.

C **Amen.**

Apostolic Greeting

P The God who reveals himself in Christ, grant you grace, and may his love be with you always.

C **And also with you.**

Prayer Of The Day

A Let us pray. God, most merciful,

C **reveal your abundance to us. Help us not to cling so closely to everything you give to us. Let us look upon all neighbors, those who love us and those who hate us, in the best possible light. Give us the courage to acknowledge our own shortcomings and invite others to affirm your strength and not ours. Amen.**

Prayers Of The Church

A Your children wander without you, God. Draw near to us as we call out to you.

(Pause for reflection)

(After each petition)

A To you, we pray.

C **Send us your blessings.**

(After the last petition)

A For each joy and pain we bring to you, and for all the needs and celebrations in the world, reveal yourself to us as life-giver, through Jesus Christ our Lord.

C **Amen.**

Offertory Prayer

A Let us pray. God of all things,

C **we offer to you these gifts, for which we give thanks. As you have blessed us by them, we return them to you, so that they may be a blessing to the ends of the earth. Use them for the creation and all its needs, through Jesus Christ, our Lord. Amen.**

Proper Preface

P It is right, our duty and our joy, that we should in all that we do give thanks and praise to you, our light, our life, and our home. As you reveal your passion to us through Jesus Christ, we marvel at how your faithfulness abounds. We respond with gladness that our Creator would dwell so closely with us. And now we join with our brothers and sisters of all times and places in the unending hymn:

Communion Welcome

P Come and eat; Christ has been poured out for you.

Post-Communion Blessing

P May the Word made flesh give you new life to proclaim the good news always.

C **Amen.**

Post-Communion Prayer

A Let us pray. Emmanuel,

C **with this bread and wine, you have once again shown us how you welcome even the least of all the saints to a place near you. Help us to be driven by your gifts to go forth in boldness and confidence to share faith and declare to the world who you truly are, our merciful Savior and Lord. Amen.**

Benediction

P May God our Father shield you, may + Christ lift your burdens, and the Holy Spirit give life to your steps.

C **Amen.**

Dismissal

P Go forward to proclaim Jesus Christ!

C **For the sake of the good news! Amen!**

Transfiguration Of Our Lord

Texts
Exodus 24:12-18
Psalm 2 alt (Psalm 99)
2 Peter 1:16-21
Matthew 17:1-9

Music Of The Day Traditional Hymns
"Immortal, Invisible, God Only Wise" (ELW834, GG12, UMH103, H423)
"Beautiful Savior/Fairest Lord Jesus" (ELW838, GG630, H384)
"Shine, Jesus, Shine" (ELW671, GG192, WOV651)
"O God, Beyond All Praising/O God, Show Mercy To Us" (ELW880, WOV797, GG341)
"O Savior, Precious Savior/O Jesus, I Have Promised" (ELW820, LBW514, GG724, UMH396)
"When Morning Gilds The Skies" (ELW853, LBW545, GG667, UMH185, H427)

Music Of The Day Contemporary Songs
"Let It Rise" by Holland Davis (ccli.com SongSelect)
"Endless Light" by Ussher/Cashwell (ccli.com SongSelect)
"Jesus Messiah" by Carson/Tomlin et al (ccli.com SongSelect)
"Fill My Cup" by Baloche et al. (ccli.com SongSelect)
"Father Of Lights" by Barnett (ccli.com SongSelect)
"Shine On Us" by Smith/Smith (ccli.com SongSelect)

Important Items
Ash Wednesday is on Wednesday of the week following the Transfiguration.

Invocation
P   Draw near to us, and shine your face upon us, + Father, Son, and Holy Spirit.
C   Amen.

Confession And Forgiveness
P   In the presence of God, let us open our hearts to renewal.
(Silence for reflection)
P   God of all ages,
C   have mercy on us. We cling to you for all the wrong reasons; we want to keep you for ourselves. Help us to let go, to become one with your passion for all of creation. Forgive us for the ways we have

separated ourselves from this purpose, and make our lives new, shining with the light of your presence through everything that we do. We ask, humbly, through Christ our Lord. Amen.

P Children of God, stand in your place at the throne of God. Your sins are forgiven, and together, one with God the + Father, Son, and Holy Spirit, we will declare the presence of God to the world.

C **Amen.**

Apostolic Greeting

P The all-consuming presence of God, create a new heart and be with you always.

C **And also with you.**

Prayer Of The Day

A Let us pray. Speak to us, Lord God,

C **and let us see you face-to-face. As your presence on the mountain changed Moses, Jesus, and the disciples, let your presence transform our very existence. Help us to live for you and to serve the gospel even as we venture down the mountain. This we pray through Jesus Christ our Lord. Amen.**

Prayers Of The Church

A Called into God's presence, let us offer prayers on behalf of the world and everything in need:

(Silence for reflection)

(After each petition)

A By your presence, Lord God,

C **hear the cries of your people.**

(After the last petition)

A We leave the weight of these prayers upon your throne, God. Remind the world that all is in your hands, and heed the call of each who turns to you, through Jesus Christ our Savior and Lord.

C **Amen.**

Offertory Prayer

A Let us pray. Bread of heaven,

C **we return to you what you have graciously given to us to tend and keep. With your blessing, use everything we can give, our very selves included, to be food for the world, giving according to each who is in need, through your Son, Jesus Christ. Amen.**

Proper Preface

P We give thanks this day, Lord, for your presence in every piece of creation. Even when it terrifies us, you offer your voice and your flesh to all of us. Though we sometimes fear, come to us always and draw out our voices, so that we may join with all the saints in your body as we sing together:

Communion Welcome

P Christ is here. Approach the table and be fed.

Post-Communion Blessing

P And now may the flesh and blood of God's very presence, Jesus Christ, fill you for all you are called to do.

C **Amen.**

Post-Communion Prayer

A Let us pray. Holy Father,

C **your sacrifice once again reminds us that you are not far off, but are a part of our every breath. By this meal, strengthen our muscles and bones to be your presence in the world for everyone we meet, through Jesus Christ our Lord. Amen.**

Benediction

P May God's face shine upon you and change your character, your actions, your identity. May the + Father, Son, and Holy Spirit dwell with you in every act.

C **Amen.**

Dismissal

A Go in peace, for the sake of the world!

C **Thanks be to God!**

Season Of Lent

Lent, pure and simple, is spring. It is a time of preparation; traditionally, in the church, it is the preparation for baptism. The lectionary follows Jesus along the path from the temptation in the wilderness to the cross at Golgotha.

The theme for Lent focuses on hearing old familiar stories in new ways. The Sundays and the Wednesdays meld together under the theme, "Conversations with Jesus." Ash Wednesday, as the start of Lent, is included with the Sunday liturgies and messages. Each week, there is a different character with whom Jesus interacts and the sermon and service should reflect a teaching imparted by the interaction.

On Wednesdays, we imagine some of the words while Jesus is praying in the garden. While not much is written of Jesus' prayers in Gethsemane, the proposed dialogues are a creative way to get at several themes of challenge for Jesus, as well as battles we face in our world today. The best way to capture this idea is to recreate the painting, *Christ in Gethsemane*, by Heinrich Hoffman. On Wednesday evenings, if possible, have the character of Jesus, robed in white, kneeling at a false rock at the front of the chancel, dramatically lit with dark background. Since the decoration for the season of Lent is typically muted, it is recommended to leave the false rock display as the symbol for all of Lent, if feasible.

In terms of plans, it has become customary to have a joint Palm and Passion Sunday a week before Easter. For the sake of this book, there are distinct plans for a unique Palm or Passion Sunday. If indeed the recent tradition is preferred, pieces can be selected from each to unite into a single joint worship experience, typically starting with the palm procession and ending with the passion narrative.

Palm Sunday should begin at the rear of the nave, with palms present and the invocation and confession and forgiveness portions of the liturgy led from there. The opening hymn would be the opportunity to process with palms waving in worship. If a dedicated Passion Sunday liturgy is chosen, the liturgy should proceed as usual, with one exception. The entire passion narrative should be read during the Eucharist to tie the traditions together between Christ continually feeding us and the work done through the cross.

Ash Wednesday

Lenten Theme: Conversations With Jesus; Dust

Texts
Joel 2:1-2, 12-17 alt (Isaiah 58:1-12)
Psalm 51:1-17
2 Corinthians 5:20b—6:10
Matthew 6:1-6, 16-21

Music Of The Day Traditional Hymns
"Beneath The Cross of Jesus" (ELW338, GG216, UMH297, H498)
"Be Thou My Vision" (ELW793, GG450, UMH451, H488)
"What Wondrous Love Is This?" (ELW666, GG215, UMH292, H439)
"Create In Me" by Hopkins (ccli.com SongSelect)
"Lamb Of God/Your Only Son" (ELW336, GG518)
"O God, Our Help In Ages Past" (ELW632, GG687, UMH117, H680)

Music Of The Day Contemporary Songs
"A Living Prayer" by Ron Block (musicnotes.com)
"You Are My King" by Foote (ccli.com SongSelect)
"Above All" by LeBlanc/Baloche (ccli.com SongSelect)
"Create In Me" by Hopkins (ccli.com SongSelect)
"Lamb Of God" by Paris (ccli.com SongSelect)
"Have Faith In God" by Bullock (ccli.com SongSelect)

Invocation
P   Blessed be the Holy Trinity, + one God, who spoke creation to existence, who called to people to walk through the wilderness, and who continues to talk through our burdens and challenges.
C   **Amen.**

Confession And Forgiveness (Psalm 51)
P   Let us confess our sins before God and one another.
(silence for reflection)
P   Have mercy on me, O God, according to your steadfast love. According to your abundant mercy, blot out my transgressions.
C   **Wash me from my iniquity, and cleanse me from my sin!**
P   For I know my transgressions, and my sin is always before me. Against you, only, have I sinned and done what is evil in your sight.
C   **Wash me from my iniquity, and cleanse me from my sin!**

P Purge me with hyssop, and I shall be clean; wash me, and I shall be whiter than the snow. Let me hear joy and gladness; let the bones that you have broken rejoice.

C **Wash me from my iniquity, and cleanse me from my sin!**

P Create in me a clean heart, O God, and renew a right spirit within me. Cast me not away from your presence, and take not your Holy Spirit from me.

C **Wash me from my iniquity, and cleanse me from my sin!**

P Restore to me the joy of your salvation, and uphold me with a willing spirit. O Lord, open my lips and my mouth will declare your praise.

C **Wash me from my iniquity, and cleanse me from my sin!**

(In some traditions, the forgiveness is not pronounced until the Maundy Thursday service; if taking this approach, make sure to explain at the opening of the service.)

P God does not delight in sacrifice, but desires a broken and contrite heart. In God's compassion, hear that your sins are washed and you are a new creation through the +life, death, and resurrection of Jesus Christ, our Lord.

C **Amen.**

(The Imposition of Ashes should follow the confession)

Apostolic Greeting

P May the voice of God, which calls, sanctifies, and redeems, be with you always.

C **And also with you.**

Prayer Of The Day

A Let us pray. Gracious God,

C **out of your love and mercy you breathed into dust the breath of life, creating us to serve you and our neighbors. Call forth our prayers and acts of kindness, and strengthen us to face our mortality with confidence in the mercy of your Son, Jesus Christ, our Savior and Lord, who lives and reigns with you and the Holy Spirit, one God, now and forever. Amen.**

Prayers Of The Church

A You spoke, and the dust moved; hear us now as we cry back to you for everyone and everything around us. *(Pause for reflection.)* From the very dirt, you formed us and all living and nonliving things; remember your declaration of the goodness of creation, and help us restore those pieces and holes that have developed over time. You breathed life into our lungs, springing us from lifelessness into relationship; mend the hearts, minds, souls, and bodies of all in need to once again feel the breath of life moving through us. You called us to return in the waters, which washed sin and gave new life. Wash the world; cleanse us from wickedness; renew us once again through your promise. You speak wisdom to those who listen. Call all who have authority and governance to repentance and reconciliation, so that we may walk together. For all the aches and divisions of the community on earth, join us with the communion of saints of all times and places as we delight in your presence for all we face each day, through Jesus Christ, our Savior and Lord.

C **Amen.**

Offertory Prayer

A   God most holy,

C   **take all that we are and all that we have to give, and transform them for your kingdom. May our very lives be of service to you and our neighbors, and may the gifts we hold briefly be used for the sake of your Son, Jesus Christ, our Lord. Amen.**

Proper Preface

P   It is our duty and joy to give you thanks always. You open yourself to all the temptations of the world, and yet remain clean. Through your grace, we have freedom from our sin and live in expectation of your triumphant return. As your glory shines through all creation, we join with the saints in their unending hymn.

Communion Welcome

P   The fast has ended. Come, eat, and live.

Post-Communion Blessing

P   May the body and blood of Jesus Christ shield and support you on your journey.

C   **Amen.**

Post-Communion Prayer

A   Let us pray. Merciful God,

C   **comfort us in all our trials by reminding us of our renewal in baptism. Give us the wisdom and strength to provide for those who are poor, pray for those in need, restrict ourselves from indulgence, and seek the treasure that does not spoil, Jesus Christ, our salvation. Amen.**

Benediction

P   May the +Word made flesh be alive in you, creating, healing, reviving all that you do for the sake of the kingdom of God.

C   **Amen.**

Dismissal

A   Go out in the world; tell the story of the good news.

C   **Thanks be to God! Amen!**

Lent 1

Lenten Theme: Conversations with Jesus; The First Disciples

Texts
Genesis 2:15-17; 3:1-7
Psalm 32
Romans 5:12-19
Matthew 4:1-11

Theme Alternative Texts
1 Samuel 3:1-11
Mark 1: 16-20

Music Of The Day Traditional Hymns And Service Music

Suggestions are given for hymns and service music in a specific order to create a cohesive flow with the Lenten theme and focus for the day. Please use your discretion and creativity to make this work for your situation and worship context.

Gathering Hymn: "Lift High The Cross/Come Christians, Follow" (ELW660, GG826, UMH159)
Gospel Welcome: "Help Us, O Lord" by Larry Olson (dakotaroadmusic.com)
Hymn of the Day: "You Are Mine/I Will Come To You In The Silence" (ELW581, GG177)
Offertory Hymn: "Create In Me" by Hopkins (ccli.com SongSelect)
Communion Hymn: "Jesus, Lamb Of God" by Linda Holcombe
Sending Hymn: "God Be With You Till We Meet Again" (ELW536, GG542, UMH672)

Music Of The Day Contemporary Songs And Service Music

Suggestions are given for songs and service music in a specific order to create a cohesive flow with the Lenten theme and focus for the day. Please use your discretion and creativity to make this work for your situation and worship context.

Gathering Song *(Music Leaders Only):* "Come To The Cross" by Smith (ccli.com SongSelect)
Song of Praise: "Let It Be Jesus" by Tomlin/Redman (ccli.com SongSelect)
Gospel Welcome: "Help Us, O Lord" by Larry Olson (dakotaroadmusic.com)
Song of the Day: "I Will Follow" by Tomlin/Ingram/Morgan (ccli.com SongSelect)
Musical Offering: "A Mighty Fortress" by Nockels (ccli.com SongSelect)
Communion Song: "Remembrance" (The Communion Song) by Maher/Redman (ccli.com SongSelect)
Sending Song *(with Congregation):* "Come To The Cross" by Smith (ccli.com SongSelect)

Invocation

P   Blessed be the Holy Trinity, + one God, who spoke creation to existence, who called to people to walk through the wilderness, who continues to talk through our burdens and challenges.

C   **Amen.**

Confession And Forgiveness (Psalm 51)

P   Let us confess our sins before God and one another.

(silence for reflection)

P   Have mercy on me, O God, according to your steadfast love; according to your abundant mercy, blot out my transgressions.

C   **Wash me from my iniquity, and cleanse me from my sin!**

P   For I know my transgressions, and my sin is always before me. Against you, only, have I sinned and done what is evil in your sight.

C   **Wash me from my iniquity, and cleanse me from my sin!**

P   Purge me with hyssop, and I shall be clean; wash me, and I shall be whiter than the snow. Let me hear joy and gladness; let the bones that you have broken rejoice.

C   **Wash me from my iniquity, and cleanse me from my sin!**

P   Create in me a clean heart, O God, and renew a right spirit within me. Cast me not away from your presence, and take not your Holy Spirit from me.

C   **Wash me from my iniquity, and cleanse me from my sin!**

P   Restore to me the joy of your salvation, and uphold me with a willing spirit. O Lord, open my lips and my mouth will declare your praise.

C   **Wash me from my iniquity, and cleanse me from my sin!**

P   God does not delight in sacrifice, but desires a broken and contrite heart. In God's compassion, hear that your sins are washed and you are a new creation through the +life, death, and resurrection of Jesus Christ, our Lord.

C   **Amen.**

Apostolic Greeting

P   May the voice of God, which calls, sanctifies, and redeems, be with you always.

C   **And also with you.**

Prayer Of The Day

A   Let us pray. Gracious Lord,

C   **by the call of your Holy Spirit, we have come to this place. Continue to speak to our hearts, so we follow your voice to all corners of our community, where by our love and service, we will proclaim the good news of your Son, Jesus Christ, our Lord. Amen.**

Prayers Of The Church

A   We return to you, Lord, as we beg on behalf of all those in need.

(Pause for reflection.)

A   Lord, speak to us who pray.

C   **send us your peace.**

(After the last petition)

A We long to hear your voice as we entrust to you all who ask for your blessing, through Jesus Christ our Lord.

C **Amen.**

Offertory Prayer

A God most holy,

C **take all that we are and all that we have to give and transform them for your kingdom. May our very lives be of service to you and our neighbors, and may the gifts we hold briefly be used for the sake of your Son, Jesus Christ, our Lord. Amen.**

Proper Preface

P It is our duty and joy to give you thanks always. You open yourself to all the temptations of the world and yet remain clean. Through your grace we have freedom from our sin and live in expectation of your triumphant return. As your glory shines through all creation we join with the saints in their unending hymn.

Communion Welcome

P The fast has ended. Come, eat, and live.

Post-Communion Blessing

P May the body and blood of Jesus Christ shield and support you on your journey.

C **Amen.**

Post-Communion Prayer

A Let us pray. Merciful God,

C **comfort us in all our trials by reminding us of our renewal in baptism. Give us the wisdom and strength to provide for those who are poor, pray for those in need, restrict ourselves from indulgence, and seek the treasure that does not spoil, Jesus Christ our salvation. Amen.**

Benediction

P May the +Word made flesh be alive in you, creating, healing, reviving all that you do for the sake of the kingdom of God.

C **Amen.**

Dismissal

A Go out in the world; tell the story of the good news.

C **Thanks be to God! Amen!**

Lent 1 — Midweek

Lenten Midweek Theme: Conversations in the Garden; Judas

Text
John 13:21-30 *(an introduction to the character of Judas)*

Music Of The Day For Lenten Midweek Worship
Most songs are taken from **Singing Our Prayer-A Companion To Holden Prayer Around The Cross** *published by Augsburg Fortress, except "Jesus, Remember Me"(WOV740) and "Stay Here"(WOV667). The songs are written in the style of the Taize worship songs: repetitious, simple, and very meditative.*

It is recommended that all songs be done in the following way: Pianist plays the entire song for an introduction; congregations sings each song four times. It is very helpful to have enough singers leading the music so that there is four-part harmony, but the songs can also be done successfully with a single song leader.

The songs used for Lenten Midweek services are the same each week, creating a simple musical framework that invites reflection and peace.

Song 1 *(following Prelude)*: "To You All Hearts Are Open"
Songs 2-3-4 *(before Readings)*: "O God, We Call"; "Let Not Your Hearts Be Troubled"; "Jesus Remember Me"
Song 5 *(before Pastor's Meditation)*: "Stay Here"
Song 6 *(after Pastor's Meditation)*: "Deep Peace"

Dialogue
Jesus: Judas…Judas?

Judas: Jesus, how did you find me here?

Jesus: Judas, I love you. You are near to me, I can find you always, though you've been keeping different company lately.

Judas: These guys? Oh, they're just some church folk I ran across while praying in the temple.

Jesus: You are bringing them to arrest me, don't you remember as we joined together in dipping the bread into wine? I knew this was coming, you were already moving in that direction.

Judas: Yeah, but….

Jesus: Judas, you are the first to fall.

(*long pause*)

Jesus: Why did you leave the group, Judas?

Judas: Jesus, I didn't leave anyone! I'm still brothers with all of you, I just…I just….

Jesus: It's okay….

Judas: I watched what you had to say about that woman and that perfume. It didn't sit right with me, to be so wasteful…so reckless. Is it so wrong to want some sort of stability? You talk about freedom, but surely even you have to have something you trust always.

Jesus: Yes, there is some….

Judas (*interrupting Jesus*): I mean, we left everything at home to follow you around. We put our whole lives in the trash and where has it gotten us? Huh? You're tap dancing all over the rules of the church, you've got the elders brooding and scheming about how to murder all of us for the chaos we've caused. Is this really what you want from us? Maybe you should've let us know at the beginning and we would've had a choice.

Jesus: You still do have a choice, Judas.

Judas (*irritated and quickly*): What choice? I feel like things are out of my hands. I'm constantly begging for food, not sure where I'm going to sleep any given night. And even when someone wants to take care of me, I'm supposed to deny everything. How is someone supposed to live, to survive going from day to day like that? (*long pause, and deep sigh, slowly*) You keep telling us God is going to fix all this — that God is moving us into this imagined place where all is well. I just don't see it…. That's why I left. That's why I had to go find someone to make things calm down a little, to restore order. I didn't want this, Jesus. I don't absolutely need the money. I'm just…scared, and trapped.

Jesus: I know, Judas. There is more to life though, than money and security.

Judas: But it's not just about the money. You're tearing apart the world. You speak all the time about peace, but at what cost?

Jesus: I know what peace will cost. It is a toll far greater than you will ever imagine. Everyone will sacrifice, and you will be blamed for many things that aren't your fault.

Judas: How do I fix it? I can't go back now, these people I'm with are pretty dangerous. I think I'm in over my head.

Jesus: No, Judas. I have made my peace with what will happen; it's time for you to do the same.

Judas: You mean to just turn you in? Surely all in our group will beat me to death as soon as they figure out what's happening.

Jesus: You don't even know what will happen when the sun rises the next day. You will see things and regret every step you made, every coin that chimes in your purse. This day will haunt you for the rest of your life.

Judas: Is there anything I can do to change it?

Jesus: No. The die is cast.

Judas: So I am trapped.

Jesus: Do you remember what I told you when I first spoke about my death when we gathered in the temple to preach and reveal the truth?

Judas: I…I can't remember.

Jesus: Everyone is trapped in sin, Judas. Everyone. Even those who claim to have never been servants to anything. To know the truth, to know that you are trapped, is part of how you become free.

Judas: I don't understand.

Jesus: You left the table tonight before I told the others that I am the way, and the truth, and the life. And as I said on that day in the temple if the Son, if the truth says you are free — then you are free.

Judas: So, Jesus, am I free?

Jesus: You are in your sin, and you will die in your sin. But never forget that phrase — I am the way, and the truth, and the life. I never stop seeking the lost coin. I never stop pursuing the sinner. I never stop breaking the chains that hold you, whether it be betrayal, greed, or even death itself.

Judas: I'm scared. The men are gathering swords, I can't stop.

Jesus: Come, Judas. I am ready. You are fulfilling your role in what needs to be.

Judas: Jesus….

Jesus: The time has come — your hour is at hand….

Lent 2

Lenten Theme: Conversations with Jesus; The Adulteress

Texts
Genesis 12:1-4a
Psalm 121
Romans 4:1-5, 13-17
John 3:1-17 alt (Matthew 17:1-9)

Theme Alternative Texts
Jonah 3:10; 4:5-11
John 8:2-11

Music Of The Day Traditional Hymns And Service Music

Suggestions are given for hymns and service music in a specific order to create a cohesive flow with the Lenten theme and focus for the day. Please use your discretion and creativity to make this work for your situation and worship context.

Gathering Hymn: "O God Of Mercy, God Of Light" (ELW714)
Gospel Welcome: "Help Us, O Lord" by Larry Olson (dakotaroadmusic.com)
Hymn of the Day: "Jesus Loves Me" (ELW595, GG188, UMH191)
Offertory Hymn: "Create In Me" by Hopkins (ccli.com SongSelect)
Communion Hymn: "Jesus, Lamb Of God" by Linda Holcombe
Sending Hymn: "Guide Me Ever Great Redeemer/Guide Me O Thou Great Jehovah" (ELW618, GG65, UMH127)

Music Of The Day Contemporary Songs And Service Music

Suggestions are given for songs and service music in a specific order to create a cohesive flow with the Lenten theme and focus for the day. Please use your discretion and creativity to make this work for your situation and worship context.

Gathering Song *(Music Leaders Only)*: "Yes, I Will" by Byrd/Hindalong (ccli.com SongSelect)
Song of Praise: "Let It Be Jesus" by Tomlin/Redman (ccli.com SongSelect)
Gospel Welcome: "Help Us, O Lord" by Larry Olson (dakotaroadmusic.com)
Song of the Day: "Amazing Love" by Foote (ccli.com SongSelect)
Musical Offering: "Jesus Loves Me" by Tomlin/Morgan/Glover (ccli.com SongSelect)
Communion Song: "Remembrance" (The Communion Song) by Maher/Redman (ccli.com SongSelect)
Sending Song *(with Congregation)*: "Yes I Will" by Byrd/Hindalong (ccli.com SongSelect)

Important Items
Saint Patrick's Day is March 17, if that is relevant to your context.

Invocation

P   Blessed be the Holy Trinity, + one God, who spoke creation to existence, who called to people to walk through the wilderness, who continues to talk through our burdens and challenges.

C   **Amen.**

Confession And Forgiveness (Psalm 51)

P   Let us confess our sins before God and one another

(silence for reflection)

P   Have mercy on me, O God, according to your steadfast love; according to your abundant mercy, blot out my transgressions.

C   **Wash me from my iniquity, and cleanse me from my sin!**

P   For I know my transgressions and my sin is always before me. Against you, only, have I sinned and done what is evil in your sight.

C   **Wash me from my iniquity, and cleanse me from my sin!**

P   Purge me with hyssop, and I shall be clean; wash me and I shall be whiter than the snow. Let me hear joy and gladness; let the bones that you have broken rejoice.

C   **Wash me from my iniquity, and cleanse me from my sin!**

P   Create in me a clean heart, O God, and renew a right spirit within me. Cast me not away from your presence and take not your Holy Spirit from me.

C   **Wash me from my iniquity, and cleanse me from my sin!**

P   Restore to me the joy of your salvation, and uphold me with a willing spirit. O Lord, open my lips and my mouth will declare your praise.

C   **Wash me from my iniquity, and cleanse me from my sin!**

P   God does not delight in sacrifice but desires a broken and contrite heart. In God's compassion hear that your sins are washed and you are a new creation through the +life, death, and resurrection of Jesus Christ our Lord.

C   **Amen.**

Apostolic Greeting

P   May the voice of God which calls, sanctifies, and redeems be with you always.

C   **And also with you.**

Prayer Of The Day

A   Let us pray. Merciful God,

C   **we come to you seeking mercy. As we open our lives, comfort us with your grace. Help us to learn honesty and hope so that we may preach the message of the truth made flesh, Jesus Christ our Lord. Amen.**

Prayers Of The Church

A   We return to you, Lord, as we beg on behalf of all those in need.

(Pause for reflection)

A   Lord, speak to us who pray.

C   **Send us your peace.**

(After the last petition)

A We long to hear your voice as we entrust to you all who ask for your blessing, through Jesus Christ our Lord.

C **Amen.**

Offertory Prayer

A God most holy,

C **take all that we are and all that we have to give and transform them for your kingdom. May our very lives be of service to you and our neighbors, and may the gifts we hold briefly be used for the sake of your Son, Jesus Christ, our Lord. Amen.**

Proper Preface

P It is our duty and joy to give you thanks always. You open yourself to all the temptations of the world and yet remain clean. Through your grace we have freedom from our sin and live in expectation of your triumphant return. As your glory shines through all creation we join with the saints in their unending hymn.

Communion Welcome

P The fast has ended. Come, eat, and live.

Post-Communion Blessing

P May the body and blood of Jesus Christ shield and support you on your journey.

C **Amen.**

Post-Communion Prayer

A Let us pray. Merciful God,

C **comfort us in all our trials by reminding us of our renewal in baptism. Give us the wisdom and strength to provide for those who are poor, pray for those in need, restrict ourselves from indulgence, and seek the treasure that does not spoil, Jesus Christ our salvation. Amen.**

Benediction

P May the +Word made flesh be alive in you, creating, healing, reviving all that you do for the sake of the kingdom of God.

C **Amen.**

Dismissal

A Go out in the world, tell the story of the good news.

C **Thanks be to God! Amen!**

Lent 2 — Midweek

Lenten Midweek Theme: Conversations In The Garden; Peter

Text
Matthew 16:13-23 *(an introduction to the character of Peter)*

Music Of The Day For Lenten Midweek Worship
Most songs are taken from **Singing Our Prayer-A Companion To Holden Prayer Around The Cross** *published by Augsburg Fortress, except "Jesus, Remember Me"(WOV740) and "Stay Here"(WOV667). The songs are written in the style of the Taize worship songs: repetitious, simple, and very meditative.*

It is recommended that all songs be done in the following way: Pianist plays the entire song for an introduction; congregation sings each song four times. It is very helpful to have enough singers leading the music so that there is four-part harmony, but the songs can also be done successfully with a single song leader.

The songs used for Lenten Midweek services are the same each week, creating a simple musical framework that invites reflection and peace.

Song 1 *(following Prelude)*: "To You All Hearts Are Open"
Songs 2-3-4 *(before Readings)*: "O God We Call"; "Let Not Your Hearts Be Troubled"; "Jesus Remember Me"
Song 5 *(before Pastor's Meditation)*: "Stay Here"
Song 6 *(after Pastor's Meditation)*: "Deep Peace"

Dialogue
Jesus: Peter

Peter [*Yawning and smacking lips*]: Yes, Lord?

Jesus: Again, Peter? Why must you always be dozing off?

Peter: I'm sorry. I had my fill at dinner. I'm just a little sleepy. But I'm good now…I'm good.

Jesus: Your endurance must be strong Peter, everyone will look to you and you will have run as far as your breath will carry you.

Peter: Lord, you said this before, but no one is as loyal to you as I am. I even stayed with you when you called me Satan. Satan! You were so upset with me that day, but I didn't walk away. Can't you see that I can take even the worst? Jesus, I am at your side forever.

Jesus: You stood by me then because you love me, Peter. But you will be accused by those who are strangers, and those you fear. When your life is threatened, you will preserve yourself.

Peter: Never.

Jesus: There is no convincing you is there? It is your passion that my Father and I saw in you which made us want you for the journey. Once you are committed, you will never give up, will you?

Peter: I don't understand, isn't that what you wanted from me when you told me to follow?

Jesus: Yes, Peter. And all of you has come along, but that does not mean you are complete. While your passion is a great gift, it is also a great weakness. It blinds you to being open to all that is going on around you.

Peter: Then tell me, Lord. I want to believe, I want to follow.

Jesus: Your life is not your own, just as mine will be handed over to those who want to control, who believe and trust in violence, who cling to power. You will have to submit to them as well.

Peter: But we are stronger than they are! They cannot overcome when we fight together, and if they do we can regroup and attack in the shadows.

Jesus: I have always sought to bring things into the light, not to hide. You still miss that there is something at work bigger than your eyes can see…bigger than your heart is willing to allow. They will come, and they will force us into servitude…they will take my life.

Peter: But Jesus we can win!

Jesus: And we will, but not on your terms. And not on mine, but on God's.

Peter: If we lose you, all we've worked for is lost. We have come so far, just look at how many people gathered to hear you preach along the side of the lake. Look at the devotion of your closest friends, we would do anything for you. We cannot lose.

Jesus: Tonight, your very fears will come true. I will be arrested. And tomorrow, I will be executed.

Peter: Jesus, no!

Jesus: And you will flee. You will flee for fear of yourself, for fear that you have lost, for all the reasons you said, you will run. It will not happen right away, but all will be revealed to you. The reason that all the things we have built will be torn down, the reason for everything you see will be opened to you. Keep your heart open, Peter, and you will see all that God has laid out.

Peter: How?! How can I believe what you're telling me if you don't trust me enough to tell me everything? If you just let me know, it would make it all easier. And maybe I wouldn't have to run.

Jesus: You wouldn't even believe then. Your heart wouldn't let you. When the day comes, remember what I have told you this day, and you will come back to the flock stronger than before.

Peter: Stronger because I was afraid? How will anyone trust me after that? I wouldn't want a deserter to come back after scampering off at the most important moment.

Jesus: You will learn that the moment isn't about you at all. There are bigger things always. There are movements you can't even sense knitting all the pieces back together. You will be a piece, Peter. You will be a rock, to which many other pieces will attach themselves; a rock that the future will come to admire not for its own strength, but for the symbol of how it stands with renewed strength.

Peter: Jesus, you aren't making any sense. Your arguments are making me tired. Let's talk about this tomorrow. We'll get back together once you get some rest and are talking in a straight line.

Jesus: Peter, there won't be a tomorrow.

Peter: Sure there will. Look, the moon is high in the sky, it's not even that cold. In fact it's a very mild night. Great for just curling up somewhere and taking a nap.

Jesus: We will talk again, Peter. Just come when you hear the call.

Peter: Grab a soft spot on the soil, Jesus. Like this one here. It'll let you unw…[*yawn*] unwind your mind a little bit. You've been too stressed lately. You need to just…just sit and…sit…[*nods off*]

Jesus: Peter….

Lent 3

Lenten Theme: Conversations With Jesus; Zacchaeus

Texts
Exodus 17:1-7
Psalm 95
Romans 5:1-11
John 4:5-42

Theme Alternative Texts
Numbers 13:17-20, 25-28, 30
Luke 19:1-10

Music Of The Day Traditional Hymns And Service Music

Suggestions are given for hymns and service music in a specific order to create a cohesive flow with the Lenten theme and focus for the day. Please use your discretion and creativity to make this work for your situation and worship context.

Gathering Hymn: "In The Cross of Christ I Glory" (ELW324, GG213, UMH295, H441)
Gospel Welcome: "Help Us, O Lord" by Larry Olson (dakotaroadmusic.com)
Hymn of the Day: "Thy Holy Wings" (ELW613, UMH502)
Offertory Hymn: "Create In Me" by Hopkins (ccli.com SongSelect)
Communion Hymn: "Jesus Lamb Of God" by Linda Holcombe
Sending Hymn: "Give To Our God Immortal Praise/From All That Dwell Below The Skies" (ELW848, UMH101)

Music Of The Day Contemporary Songs And Service Music

Suggestions are given for songs and service music in a specific order to create a cohesive flow with the Lenten theme and focus for the day. Please use your discretion and creativity to make this work for your situation and worship context.

Gathering Song *(Music Leaders Only):* "This Is Amazing Grace" by Wickham (ccli.com SongSelect)
Song of Praise: "Let It Be Jesus" by Tomlin/Redman (ccli.com SongSelect)
Gospel Welcome: "Help Us O Lord" by Larry Olson (dakotaroadmusic.com)
Song of the Day: "How Great Is Our" God by Tomlin/Reeves/Cash (ccli.com SongSelect)
Musical Offering: "Oceans" by Crocker/Houston/Ligthelm (ccli.com SongSelect)
Communion Song: "You Are Holy" by Paris (ccli.com SongSelect)
Sending Song *(with Congregation):* "This Is Amazing Grace" by Wickham (ccli.com SongSelect)

Important Items

Today is the festival for Saint Joseph, guardian of our Lord.

Invocation

P Blessed be the Holy Trinity, + one God, who spoke creation to existence, who called to people to walk through the wilderness, who continues to talk through our burdens and challenges.

C **Amen.**

Confession And Forgiveness (Psalm 51)

P Let us confess our sins before God and one another.

(silence for reflection)

P Have mercy on me, O God, according to your steadfast love; according to your abundant mercy, blot out my transgressions.

C **Wash me from my iniquity, and cleanse me from my sin!**

P For I know my transgressions and my sin is always before me. Against you, only, have I sinned and done what is evil in your sight.

C **Wash me from my iniquity, and cleanse me from my sin!**

P Purge me with hyssop, and I shall be clean; wash me and I shall be whiter than the snow. Let me hear joy and gladness; let the bones that you have broken rejoice.

C **Wash me from my iniquity, and cleanse me from my sin!**

P Create in me a clean heart, O God, and renew a right spirit within me. Cast me not away from your presence and take not your Holy Spirit from me.

C **Wash me from my iniquity, and cleanse me from my sin!**

P Restore to me the joy of your salvation, and uphold me with a willing spirit. O Lord, open my lips and my mouth will declare your praise.

C **Wash me from my iniquity, and cleanse me from my sin!**

P God does not delight in sacrifice but desires a broken and contrite heart. In God's compassion hear that your sins are washed and you are a new creation through the +life, death, and resurrection of Jesus Christ our Lord.

C **Amen.**

Apostolic Greeting

P May the voice of God which calls, sanctifies, and redeems be with you always.

C **And also with you.**

Prayer Of The Day

A Let us pray. Glorious Father,

C **you send your light to the world to push back the darkness. Remove the shade from our eyes so that we may see clearly the world around us and indeed our very selves, through Jesus Christ our Lord. Amen.**

Prayers Of The Church

A We return to you, Lord, as we beg on behalf of all those in need.

(Pause for reflection)

A Lord, speak to us who pray,

C **send us your peace.**

(After the last petition)

A   We long to hear your voice as we entrust to you all who ask for your blessing, through Jesus Christ our Lord.

C   **Amen.**

Offertory Prayer

A   God most holy,

C   **take all that we are and all that we have to give and transform them for your kingdom. May our very lives be of service to you and our neighbors, and may the gifts we hold briefly be used for the sake of your Son, Jesus Christ, our Lord. Amen.**

Proper Preface

P   It is our duty and joy to give you thanks always. You open yourself to all the temptations of the world and yet remain clean. Through your grace we have freedom from our sin and live in expectation of your triumphant return. As your glory shines through all creation we join with the saints in their unending hymn.

Communion Welcome

P   The fast has ended. Come, eat, and live.

Post-Communion Blessing

P   May the body and blood of Jesus Christ shield and support you on your journey.

C   **Amen.**

Post-Communion Prayer

A   Let us pray. Merciful God,

C   **comfort us in all our trials by reminding us of our renewal in baptism. Give us the wisdom and strength to provide for those who are poor, pray for those in need, restrict ourselves from indulgence, and seek the treasure that does not spoil, Jesus Christ our salvation. Amen.**

Benediction

P   May the +Word made flesh be alive in you, creating, healing, reviving all that you do for the sake of the kingdom of God.

C   **Amen.**

Dismissal

A   Go out in the world, tell the story of the good news.

C   **Thanks be to God! Amen!**

Lenten Midweek Theme: Conversations In The Garden; Pilate

Text
John 18: 28-38 *(an introduction to the character of Pontius Pilate)*

Music Of The Day For Lenten Midweek Worship
Most songs are taken from **Singing Our Prayer-A Companion To Holden Prayer Around The Cross** *published by Augsburg Fortress, except "Jesus, Remember Me"(WOV740) and "Stay Here"(WOV667). The songs are written in the style of the Taize worship songs: repetitious, simple, and very meditative.*

It is recommended that all songs be done in the following way: Pianist plays the entire song for an introduction; congregation sings each song four times. It is very helpful to have enough singers leading the music so that there is four-part harmony, but the songs can also be done successfully with a single song leader.

The songs used for Lenten Midweek services are the same each week, creating a simple musical framework that invites reflection and peace.

Song 1 *(following Prelude)*: "To You All Hearts Are Open"
Songs 2-3-4 *(before Readings)*: "O God We Call"; "Let Not Your Hearts Be Troubled"; "Jesus Remember Me"
Song 5 *(before Pastor's Meditation)*: "Stay Here"
Song 6 *(after Pastor's Meditation)*: "Deep Peace"

Dialogue
Jesus: Pilate.

Pilate: Hmm. Do I know you? Your voice is not one I recognize. How do you come to me?

Jesus: We have not met, though we will soon. I am called Jesus.

Pilate: The man from the backwaters of Galilee? What town was it, Nazareth?

Jesus: Yes.

Pilate: Yes, your reputation precedes you, Jesus. You've been making quite a stir in the lower circuits. You're quite the troublemaker aren't you?

Jesus: I come bringing light to the world, but the world cannot stand the light. Those that resist fight against what is inevitable, and against what would release them from their chains.

Pilate: Release them? Chains? What exactly are you trying to do, sir? The people of this land do not need to be freed from anything. Rome gives them shelter, water, food, safety. They are more free now then they have ever been. I should hope that you do not come to trouble me with your simple concerns. I don't have time for annoying flies.

Jesus: Actually, I come not on my own behalf, but for my Father who sent me.

Pilate: Your Father? Is he anyone of importance?

Jesus: You have not met Him either....

Pilate: Then quit wasting my time. I can't be bothered with all manners of trivial activity. I have my own people to govern, return to your home and bother someone there.

Jesus: I want to speak to you about your people.

Pilate: Have they elected you as some sort of representative? Why would you speak to me about them if you have no place here?

Jesus: I have no home anywhere. I come with the voice of God to preach truth to your power.

Pilate: God?! You mean Caesar sent you.

Jesus: If I would have meant Caesar, I would have said Caesar. Do you fear Caesar?

Pilate: I am left alone to govern here. There is nothing here for me to fear as long as I keep fear among the people, and they fall in line.

Jesus: Who gave you the authority to govern?

Pilate: I have no patience for your philosophy. Leave me.

Jesus: Who gave you the authority to govern?

Pilate: I was appointed. There is a system in place, and I moved through it. One step at a time I climbed, and I will move through to the next step soon. This is the Roman way, as it has always been.

Jesus: Indeed, you have been appointed, but by a force you have no control and no vision of. You are in this place as a torturer, as a murderer. You will be called to account for these tasks, but first....

Pilate: You accuse me? You try my patience, Jesus! What would you know of power, of authority? What would you know about control? You who grew up nowhere, who has settled nowhere, who has nothing, and who means nothing. You, just as before this day, will fade to oblivion where the countless before you have been forgotten.

Jesus: Tomorrow, your perception of all things will change. Your power will be challenged. Even what you think you control will turn against you and rule over you.

Pilate: Are you going to gather the people against me? I will slaughter you and your "army."

Jesus: You will learn much about the power you have, and the power you don't have. While not even holding a sword, power will be wrested away from you. Your own people will follow their own wills and bend you to their desire.

Pilate: My people would not turn their heads away when I speak.

Jesus: You call them your people. You use those words, "my people," but they have no value, they are of no worth to you. They are at best an annoyance. Do you treat everything you call yours with such disdain? Weren't you appointed to serve these people? And are they here for your own ambitions?

Pilate: I am free to do with what is mine as I choose.

Jesus: If this is what you truly believe, then they are already not your own. You try to keep them from realizing this by fear, and by might. The moment they don't respect you, your world will crumble. You should relate to what is yours with love and respect and service. Only in this will they be yours, and you will belong to them.

Pilate: You and I have nothing further to say today, Jesus. I will see you tomorrow. And we shall see if what you say is true.

Jesus: I AM the truth.

Pilate: (*hmph*)

Lent 4

Lenten Theme: Conversations With Jesus; The Syrophoenician Woman

Texts
1 Samuel 16:1-13
Psalm 23
Ephesians 5:8-14
John 9:1-41

> *Theme Alternative Texts*
> Exodus 32:7-14
> Mark 7:24-30

Music Of The Day Traditional Hymns And Service Music

Suggestions are given for hymns and service music in a specific order to create a cohesive flow with the Lenten theme and focus for the day. Please use your discretion and creativity to make this work for your situation and worship context.

Gathering Hymn: "O For A Thousand Tongues To Sing" (ELW886, GG610, UMH57, H493)
Gospel Welcome: "Help Us, O Lord" by Larry Olson (dakotaroadmusic.com)
Hymn of the Day: "Beautiful Savior/Fairest Lord Jesus" (ELW838, GG630, H384)
Offertory Hymn: "Create In Me" by Hopkins (ccli.com SongSelect)
Communion Hymn: "Jesus, Lamb Of God" by Linda Holcombe
Sending Hymn: "Blessed Assurance" (ELW638, GG839, UMH369)

Music Of The Day Contemporary Songs And Service Music

Suggestions are given for songs and service music in a specific order to create a cohesive flow with the Lenten theme and focus for the day. Please use your discretion and creativity to make this work for your situation and worship context.

Gathering Song *(Music Leaders Only):* "Living Sacrifice" by Engle (ccli.com SongSelect)
Song of Praise: "Let It Be Jesus" by Tomlin/Redman (ccli.com SongSelect)
Gospel Welcome: "Help Us, O Lord" by Larry Olson (dakotaroadmusic.com)
Song of the Day: "Holy, Holy, Holy" arr. by Morgan (ccli.com SongSelect)
Musical Offering: "Lord Have Mercy" by Steve Merkel (ccli.com SongSelect)
Communion Song: "You Are Holy" by Paris (ccli.com SongSelect)
Sending Song *(with Congregation):* "Living Sacrifice" by Engle (ccli.com SongSelect)

Invocation

P Blessed be the Holy Trinity, + one God, who spoke creation to existence, who called to people to walk through the wilderness, who continues to talk through our burdens and challenges

C **Amen.**

Confession And Forgiveness (Psalm 51)

P Let us confess our sins before God and one another.

(silence for reflection)

P Have mercy on me, O God, according to your steadfast love; according to your abundant mercy, blot out my transgressions.

C **Wash me from my iniquity, and cleanse me from my sin!**

P For I know my transgressions and my sin is always before me. Against you, only, have I sinned and done what is evil in your sight.

C **Wash me from my iniquity, and cleanse me from my sin!**

P Purge me with hyssop, and I shall be clean; wash me and I shall be whiter than the snow. Let me hear joy and gladness; let the bones that you have broken rejoice.

C **Wash me from my iniquity, and cleanse me from my sin!**

P Create in me a clean heart, O God, and renew a right spirit within me. Cast me not away from your presence and take not your Holy Spirit from me.

C **Wash me from my iniquity, and cleanse me from my sin!**

P Restore to me the joy of your salvation, and uphold me with a willing spirit. O Lord, open my lips and my mouth will declare your praise.

C **Wash me from my iniquity, and cleanse me from my sin!**

P God does not delight in sacrifice but desires a broken and contrite heart. In God's compassion hear that your sins are washed and you are a new creation through the +life, death, and resurrection of Jesus Christ our Lord.

C **Amen.**

Apostolic Greeting

P May the voice of God which calls, sanctifies, and redeems be with you always.

C **And also with you.**

Prayer Of The Day

A Let us pray. Ever-present God,

C **draw us once again to you. Help us to understand that you are not done with us yet, and that as long as there is air in our lungs there is work to be done. This we pray through Jesus Christ our Lord. Amen.**

Prayers Of The Church

A We return to you, Lord, as we beg on behalf of all those in need.

(pause for reflection)

A Lord, speak to us who pray.

C **Send us your peace.**

(After the last petition)

A We long to hear your voice as we entrust to you all who ask for your blessing, through Jesus Christ our Lord.

C **Amen.**

Offertory Prayer

A God most holy,

C **take all that we are and all that we have to give and transform them for your kingdom. May our very lives be of service to you and our neighbors, and may the gifts we hold briefly be used for the sake of your Son, Jesus Christ, our Lord. Amen.**

Proper Preface

P It is our duty and joy to give you thanks always. You open yourself to all the temptations of the world and yet remain clean. Through your grace we have freedom from our sin and live in expectation of your triumphant return. As your glory shines through all creation we join with the saints in their unending hymn.

Communion Welcome

P The fast has ended. Come, eat, and live.

Post-Communion Blessing

P May the body and blood of Jesus Christ shield and support you on your journey.

C **Amen.**

Post-Communion Prayer

A Let us pray. Merciful God,

C **comfort us in all our trials by reminding us of our renewal in baptism. Give us the wisdom and strength to provide for those who are poor, pray for those in need, restrict ourselves from indulgence, and seek the treasure that does not spoil, Jesus Christ our salvation. Amen.**

Benediction

P May the +Word made flesh be alive in you, creating, healing, reviving all that you do for the sake of the kingdom of God.

C **Amen.**

Dismissal

A Go out in the world, tell the story of the good news.

C **Thanks be to God! Amen!**

Lent 4 — Midweek

Lenten Midweek Theme: Conversations In The Garden; Mary

Texts
Luke 1:46-55 *(an introduction to the character of Mary)*

Music Of The Day For Lenten Midweek Worship
Most songs are taken from **Singing Our Prayer-A Companion To Holden Prayer Around The Cross** *published by Augsburg Fortress, except "Jesus, Remember Me"(WOV740) and "Stay Here"(WOV667). The songs are written in the style of the Taize worship songs: repetitious, simple, and very meditative.*

It is recommended that all songs be done in the following way: Pianist plays the entire song for an introduction; congregation sings each song four times. It is very helpful to have enough singers leading the music so that there is four-part harmony, but the songs can also be done successfully with a single song leader.

The songs used for Lenten Midweek services are the same each week, creating a simple musical framework that invites reflection and peace.

Song 1 *(following Prelude)*: "To You All Hearts Are Open"
Songs 2-3-4 *(before Readings)*: "O God We Call"; "Let Not Your Hearts Be Troubled"; "Jesus Remember Me"
Song 5 *(before Pastor's Meditation)*: "Stay Here"
Song 6 *(after Pastor's Meditation)*: "Deep Peace"

Dialogue
Jesus: Mother?

Mary: Jesus, where have you gone? I've been following for what seems like ages since you were run out of town. I've been excited to hear how the people speak of you.

Jesus: Life has gotten a bit out of hand lately. This mission has picked up more and more steam lately, it's taken me in and out of homes around the country. At the moment I'm praying.

Mary: You always have been good about your prayer, Jesus. I'm glad to see you've kept your priorities in talking to our Lord even when things get hectic.

Jesus: It's not just being busy, the world is about to get really ugly.

Mary: What's wrong?

Jesus: It's not the time. I'd rather not talk about it until later.

Mary: Son, let's talk now. We haven't had a chance to talk, and I don't know when we're going to get another time.

Jesus: I don't think you're ready, it's not what you think.

Mary: I think you're forgetting who raised you. Who was it that changed your diapers, hmm? When you would run off to the temple, who calmed Joseph down? I've been there when you scraped your knees, when you hammered your thumb, every time something bad happened to you, I've been there to pick you up. What could be so bad that you think I'm not ready?

Jesus: I… they're going to kill me, Mother.

Mary: What?

Jesus: Do you remember all the stories you used to tell me, Mother? Of angels and lights, of kings, and of majestic voices and songs? Of Aunt Elizabeth and John?

Mary: Of course I do, but what does that have to do with…

Jesus: I remember all the stories you used to tell me at bedtime, of that first time in the temple where everyone flocked to you, and that one old man told you that his eyes saw the salvation of the world.

Mary: Yes, but…

Jesus: He told you that a sword would pierce your soul. Do you remember that story?

Mary: I can't…

Jesus: Tomorrow that prophecy will come true.

Mary: What are you saying? I saw the people when you came into Jerusalem. They were in a frenzy. All ecstatic, crying out to God in thanks! All singing your praise! How on earth could you possibly be in danger when everyone would throw their lives in the way to protect you?

Jesus: Everyone will leave me.

Mary: That makes no sense.

Jesus: Mother, everyone will.

Mary: No, I won't.

Jesus: No, mother. You will always love me, and look after me. But when the whole city rises up, you won't be able to stand. You will have to watch as they torture and murder me.

Mary: No!

Jesus: It's been written! There is no other way.

Mary: There's always another way! What if … what if we leave tonight? We could get out of town, wait until all the riots have settled. We could hide for a while just you and me. We'll come back to everyone when the excitement is over. Then you can go back to teaching …

Jesus: No.

Mary: But what about the Romans? We can make sure that they protect you, say that you are coming to help to teach all the Jews about peace and love. Surely they would be willing to listen to you!

Jesus: The Romans will lead my execution.

Mary: Then fight! Do something! Let them take me instead! I'll take the blame for the whole thing, let me! I can't lose you!

Jesus: …

Mary: There just has to be something else.

Jesus: I've tried every other way. This must happen. God our Father has spoken and we all must follow into this plan.

Mary: I just don't understand why.

Jesus: Mother, my heart aches for you. You shouldn't have to watch this, but I need you to still follow. I need you to be there through everything.

Mary: I don't know how I can. How can you ask me to do this?

Jesus: Your love, your devotion to me and to God will carry you through. Just don't turn away. You will sing again before all is done.

Mary: I can't ever imagine a future when I will smile again if what you say is true.

Jesus: You will be a beacon of hope to many. I will ask our Father if there is any way, but I need you to be there.

Mary: I have seen you through every step of your life. I won't leave you now, Jesus. But give me something to hold on to. Some reason to see this through as you say.

Jesus: All that you endure tomorrow will make sense, and will lead to a better future for all.

Mary: I will be there. God help me, I will be there.

Jesus: Thank you, for all you are and will be.

Mary: I love you, my son. More than anything in the world.

Jesus: I love you, Mom.

Lent 5

Lenten Theme: Conversations With Jesus; Nicodemus

Texts
Psalm 118:1-2, 19-29
Matthew 21:1-11

> *Theme Alternative Texts*
> 1 Corinthians 13:9-12
> John 3:1-16

Music Of The Day Traditional Hymns And Service Music

Suggestions are given for hymns and service music in a specific order to create a cohesive flow with the Lenten theme and focus for the day. Please use your discretion and creativity to make this work for your situation and worship context.

Gathering Hymn: "Come Thou Fount of Every Blessing" (ELW807, GG475, UMH400, H686)
Gospel Welcome: "Help Us O Lord" by Larry Olson (dakotaroadmusic.com)
Hymn of the Day: "Lord of All Hopefulness" (ELW765, GG683, H482)
Offertory Hymn: "Create In Me" by Hopkins (ccli.com SongSelect)
Communion Hymn: "Jesus Lamb Of God" by Linda Holcombe
Sending Hymn: "Go, My Children, With My Blessing/God That Madest Earth And Heaven" (ELW543, GG547, UMH688)

Music Of The Day Contemporary Songs And Service Music

Suggestions are given for songs and service music in a specific order to create a cohesive flow with the Lenten theme and focus for the day. Please use your discretion and creativity to make this work for your situation and worship context.

Gathering Song *(Music Leaders Only):* "What A Friend We Have In Jesus" *(swing style)* (musicnotes.com)
Song of Praise: "Let It Be Jesus" by Tomlin/Redman (ccli.com SongSelect)
Gospel Welcome: "Help Us, O Lord" by Larry Olson (dakotaroadmusic.com)
Song of the Day: "Jesus Messiah" by Carson/Tomlin et al (ccli.com SongSelect)
Musical Offering: "Hold Me Close" by Paris (ccli.com SongSelect)
Communion Song: "Jesus, Lamb Of God" by Linda Holcombe
Sending Song *(with Congregation):* "What A Friend We Have In Jesus" *(Swing style)* (musicnotes.com)

Invocation

P   Blessed be the Holy Trinity, + one God, who spoke creation to existence, who called to people to walk through the wilderness, who continues to talk through our burdens and challenges.

C   Amen.

Confession And Forgiveness (Psalm 51)

P   Let us confess our sins before God and one another.

(silence for reflection)

P   Have mercy on me, O God, according to your steadfast love; according to your abundant mercy, blot out my transgressions.

C   **Wash me from my iniquity, and cleanse me from my sin!**

P   For I know my transgressions and my sin is always before me. Against you, only, have I sinned and done what is evil in your sight.

C   **Wash me from my iniquity, and cleanse me from my sin!**

P   Purge me with hyssop, and I shall be clean; wash me and I shall be whiter than the snow. Let me hear joy and gladness; let the bones that you have broken rejoice.

C   **Wash me from my iniquity, and cleanse me from my sin!**

P   Create in me a clean heart, O God, and renew a right spirit within me. Cast me not away from your presence and take not your Holy Spirit from me.

C   **Wash me from my iniquity, and cleanse me from my sin!**

P   Restore to me the joy of your salvation, and uphold me with a willing spirit. O Lord, open my lips and my mouth will declare your praise.

C   **Wash me from my iniquity, and cleanse me from my sin!**

P   God does not delight in sacrifice but desires a broken and contrite heart. In God's compassion hear that your sins are washed and you are a new creation through the +life, death, and resurrection of Jesus Christ our Lord.

C   **Amen.**

Apostolic Greeting

P   May the voice of God which calls, sanctifies, and redeems be with you always.

C   **And also with you.**

Prayer Of The Day

A   Let us pray. God most wise,

C   **challenge our thoughts and our wills. Open us to new understandings of who you are and how you embrace the world. Keep our hearts and minds close to you as we pray through your Son Jesus Christ our Lord. Amen.**

Prayers Of The Church

A   We return to you, Lord, as we beg on behalf of all those in need.

(pause for reflection)

A   Lord, speak to us who pray.

C   **Send us your peace.**

(after the last petition)

A   We long to hear your voice as we entrust to you all who ask for your blessing, through Jesus Christ our Lord.

C   **Amen.**

Offertory Prayer

A God most holy,

C **take all that we are and all that we have to give and transform them for your kingdom. May our very lives be of service to you and our neighbors, and may the gifts we hold briefly be used for the sake of your Son, Jesus Christ, our Lord. Amen.**

Proper Preface

P It is our duty and joy to give you thanks always. You open yourself to all the temptations of the world and yet remain clean. Through your grace we have freedom from our sin and live in expectation of your triumphant return. As your glory shines through all creation we join with the saints in their unending hymn.

Communion Welcome

P The fast has ended. Come, eat, and live.

Post-Communion Blessing

P May the body and blood of Jesus Christ shield and support you on your journey.

C **Amen.**

Post-Communion Prayer

A Let us pray. Merciful God,

C **comfort us in all our trials by reminding us of our renewal in baptism. Give us the wisdom and strength to provide for those who are poor, pray for those in need, restrict ourselves from indulgence, and seek the treasure that does not spoil, Jesus Christ our salvation. Amen.**

Benediction

P May the +Word made flesh be alive in you, creating, healing, reviving all that you do for the sake of the kingdom of God.

C **Amen.**

Dismissal

A Go out in the world, tell the story of the good news.

C **Thanks be to God! Amen!**

Lent 5 — Midweek

Lenten Midweek Theme: Conversations In The Garden; God The Father

Text
Revelation 21:1-7 *(an introduction to the character of God the Father)*

Music Of The Day For Lenten Midweek Worship
Most songs are taken from **Singing Our Prayer-A Companion To Holden Prayer Around The Cross** *published by Augsburg Fortress, except "Jesus, Remember Me"(WOV740) and "Stay Here"(WOV667). The songs are written in the style of the Taize worship songs: repetitious, simple, and very meditative.*

It is recommended that all songs be done in the following way: Pianist plays the entire song for an **introduction***; congregation sings each song four times. It is very helpful to have enough singers leading the music so* **that there is** *four-part harmony, but the songs can also be done successfully with a single song leader.*

The songs used for Lenten Midweek services are the same each week, creating a simple musical framework that invites reflection and peace.

Song 1 *(following Prelude)*: "To You All Hearts Are Open"
Songs 2-3-4 *(before Readings):* "O God We Call"; "Let Not Your Hearts Be Troubled"; "Jesus Remember Me"
Song 5 *(before Pastor's Meditation)*: "Stay Here"
Song 6 *(after Pastor's Meditation)*: "Deep Peace"

Dialogue
Jesus *(increasingly frantic)*: Abba? Father, it's me. I'm nearly there. I've walked all this way, the people I've met, the stories I've shared, the tears I've cried with them. I love them, Father. I worried when I came that I would see them only for their shortcomings. But it's different living with them, to feel their struggles, to step with them through the ashes of their life, to feel the flesh and the burdens that come with it, it's unlike anything I ever could have expected. I'm sure you feel it now too. It's not just understanding who they are, but it's being joined with them. In offering them a piece of me I've taken them into myself. We are one... and I think that's why I'm worried. I've been telling them for a few weeks now that my time is short, and it's making them concerned. I don't know... I want to be with them always... I want to believe my time with them has mattered, is there another way? Can't I find a way to stay with them longer? Maybe more time will lead to more followers. Time is running out and...

God: Son.

Jesus: I know, I'm sorry. I just...

God: Come and sit with me.

Jesus: I… Okay. But they're coming to take me away soon.

God: We have all the time in the world to talk, let's dwell together a while. Don't you remember when we spoke all of this into existence? When we counted days not by hours or by sunshine but by forming and shaping from nothing. There was no time, no schedule — we were all there was and all there ever would be.

Jesus: It's so hard to see that here. There's this never-ending push or pull to the next task and the next day.

God: So what happens if that goes away? Would you feel at rest if there was nothing to look forward to?

Jesus: Well no, it would feel kind of empty.

God: So you just want to know that there's something else?

Jesus: Maybe. There are things I can see, and things I know are coming but I don't always know what to make of being able to see. Some of it is terrifying.

God: What makes you so afraid? Pain? Death?

Jesus: It is a horrible fate to face. But, no. I think what makes me most afraid is humanity itself. There's a darkness here always hiding just around the corner. There's this sense of the other shoe just waiting to drop always. There's never a hope of what might be — only a concern about what might happen, it seems to swallow everything.

God: Do you not believe in the future?

Jesus: I believe, but I still wonder if there's a different way. Tomorrow, that moment when the darkness wins, when I look out and see nothing but shadow, where will you be? When I feel that absolute abandonment, I think that moment scares me the most, to feel your absence.

God: You know that it is necessary. I am there, you must dive into the abyss to draw those who exist in our absence back home. We will join back together soon, there is no way for us to really be separate. Where you go, I am there.

Jesus: I guess I just need the reassurance. I trust in your will for me, even if sometimes I don't get the whole picture. I thank you for this mission. It has changed the reality of the world. These people will be forever closer to us. I wish it would set in right away, but in the end, all will know.

God: In the end, as in the beginning. I am.

Jesus: We are.

Palm Sunday

Lenten Theme: Conversations With Jesus; The Crowd At Jerusalem

Texts
Psalm 118:1-2, 19-29
Matthew 21:1-11

Theme Alternative Texts
Zechariah 9:9-13
Philippians 2:1-11

Music Of The Day Traditional Hymns And Service Music

Suggestions are given for hymns and service music in a specific order to create a cohesive flow with the Lenten theme and focus for the day. We end this service with "Beneath The Cross of Jesus," the hymn with which we started Lent with on Ash Wednesday. Please use your discretion and creativity to make this work for your situation and worship context.

"Gathering Hymn: All Glory Laud and Honor/Thou Art The King of Israel" (ELW344, GG196, UMH280, H154)

"Gospel Welcome: Help Us O Lord" by Larry Olson (dakotaroadmusic.com)

Hymn of the Day: "When I Survey The Wondrous Cross" (ELW803, GG223, UMH298)

Offertory Hymn: "Create In Me" by Hopkins (ccli.com SongSelect)

Communion Hymn: "Jesus Lamb Of God" by Linda Holcombe

Sending Hymn: "Beneath The Cross of Jesus" (ELW338, GG216, UMH297, H498)

Music Of The Day Contemporary Songs And Service Music

Suggestions are given for songs and service music in a specific order to create a cohesive flow with the Lenten theme and focus for the day. Please use your discretion and creativity to make this work for your situation and worship context.

Gathering Song *(Music Leaders Only):* "These Thousand Hills" by Atwell/Blackburn/Davison (ccli.com SongSelect)

Song of Praise: "Hosanna" by Christensen/Orsini (ccli.com SongSelect)

Gospel Welcome: "Help Us O Lord" by Larry Olson (dakotaroadmusic.com)

Song of the Day: "Weeping Over Jerusalem" by Olson (ccli.com SongSelect)

Musical Offering: "Above All" by LeBlanc (ccli.com SongSelect)

Communion Song: "Jesus Lamb Of God" by Linda Holcombe

Sending Song *(with Congregation):* "These Thousand Hills" by Atwell/Blackburn/Davison (ccli.com SongSelect)

Invocation

P Save us from our sin, triumph over evil and all that works against you, Father, Son, and Holy Spirit.

C Amen.

Confession And Forgiveness

P Let us offer to God all of who we are; strengths and weaknesses;
(silence for reflection)

P God most high,

C we confess to you where we have misunderstood. We have not revered you as messiah. We have pushed you into simple explanations which do not reflect your majesty. In so doing we have severed ties with you, with our neighbors, and ourselves. Forgive us, and call us again to worship you for who you are and not who we want you to be. Amen.

P God did not come to lord power over us, but to serve. By the mercy of + Christ your sins are forgiven. Live in new relationship with the Lord your God.

C Amen.

Apostolic Greeting

P May the triumphant king who comes to us grant you mercy and peace this day.

C Amen.

Prayer Of The Day

A Let us pray. Come, holy Messiah.

C Let our hearts cry out in joy for your presence. So teach and guide us that we may experience the power of your death and resurrection as permeating all areas of our life; that our celebration may be a sign of our whole lives renewed by your arrival. In your holy name we pray. Amen.

Prayers Of The Church

A As followers of our God and King, let us pray on behalf of those who need Christ's presence
(Silence for reflection)
(After each petition)

A Hear our prayer, Lord.

C And come to our help.
(After the last petition)

A Enter in to all parts of our life, renewing and creating all things through your Son, Jesus Christ our Lord.

C Amen.

Offertory Prayer

A Let us pray. Holy Father,

C we offer to you worship, praise, and thanks for all you have given. In response, take what we have given and use it for the entire creation, that we may join with you in the fight against evil and all harm. Through Jesus Christ our Lord. Amen.

Proper Preface

P It is our duty and joy to give you thanks and praise. You ride victorious into this world not as a tyrant, but as a peasant. So instill in us this sense of service to the world that we may join with the saints of every time and place as we join in the eternal hymn:

Communion Welcome

P Approach the throne of glory and share in Christ's gifts for you.

Post-Communion Blessing

P May you be strengthened by the body and blood of Christ for your calling and service to the world.

C **Amen.**

Post-Communion Prayer

A Let us pray, merciful God,

C **we follow you to the ends of the earth. As you nourish us for the journey, use this moment of grace to help us live in new relationship with all of our brothers and sisters and invite them into the way, the truth, and the life. Amen.**

Benediction

P May God, + Father, Son, and Holy Spirit ease your burdens and inspire you to new life for the sake of conquering sin and death in the world.

C **Amen.**

Dismissal

A Go out this day in joy and peace

C **For the sake of our king. Amen!**

Passion Sunday

Lenten Theme: Conversations With God; The Father

<u>Texts</u>
Isaiah 50:4-9a
Psalm 31:9-16
Philippians 2:5-11
Matthew 26:14-27:66 alt. (Matthew 27:11-54, it is recommended to use the longer reading for Communion)

Music of the Day Traditional Hymns and Service Music
Suggestions are given for hymns and service music in a specific order to create a cohesive flow with the Lenten theme and focus for the day. We end this service with "Beneath The Cross of Jesus," the hymn we started Lent with on Ash Wednesday. Please use your discretion and creativity to make this work for your situation and worship context.
"Gathering Hymn: All Glory Laud and Honor/Thou Art The King of Israel (ELW344, GG196, UMH280, H154)
Gospel Welcome: "Help Us O Lord" by Larry Olson (dakotaroadmusic.com)
Hymn of the Day: "When I Survey The Wondrous Cross" (ELW803, GG223, UMH298)
Offertory Hymn: "Create In Me" by Hopkins (ccli.com SongSelect)
Communion Hymn: "Jesus Lamb Of God" by Linda Holcombe
Sending Hymn: "Beneath The Cross of Jesus" (ELW338, GG216, UMH297, H498)

Music of the Day Contemporary Songs and Service Music
Suggestions are given for songs and service music in a specific order to create a cohesive flow with the Lenten theme and focus for the day. Please use your discretion and creativity to make this work for your situation and worship context.
Gathering Song *(Music Leaders Only):* "These Thousand Hills" by Atwell/Blackburn/Davison (ccli.com SongSelect)
Song of Praise: "Hosanna" by Christensen/Orsini (ccli.com SongSelect)
Gospel Welcome: "Help Us O Lord" by Larry Olson (dakotaroadmusic.com)
Song of the Day: "Weeping Over Jerusalem" by Olson (ccli.com SongSelect)
Musical Offering: "Above All" by LeBlanc (ccli.com SongSelect)
Communion Song: "Jesus Lamb Of God" by Linda Holcombe
Sending Song *(With Congregation):* "These Thousand Hills" by Atwell/Blackburn/Davison (ccli.com SongSelect)

Invocation
P   As we witness the cost of our sin, draw near to us + Father, Son, and Holy Spirit so that we may still know of your love.

C Amen.

Confession & Forgiveness

P Let us stand at the foot of the cross, bearing witness to our sin;

(silence for reflection)

P Lord lifted up,

C **Our sins form the nails which hold you to the tree, and yet you bear it gladly. Hold our hearts captive to your love, so that we may not trust in our own ability to be better people, but may rely on your strength even in spite of our betrayal. Amen.**

P God sent His only Son so that the world may be reconciled through the crucifixion and resurrection of Jesus the Christ. By the compassion of our God + your sins are forgiven this day.

C Amen.

Apostolic Greeting

P May the God whose love knows no end grant you peace this day.

C Amen.

Prayer of the Day

A Let us pray. Pour out your love, O God,

C **We hear again the story of your passion for your creation. In the cross of Christ guide us to see that you hate nothing you have created, even a creation that does not know you. Amen.**

Prayers of the Church

A As the first witnesses of God's love let us bring the burdens of others to the throne of grace;

(Silence for reflection)

(After each petition)

A Stay near us, Lord

C **And come to our help**

(After the last petition)

A Let your love pour out to all those we raise before you this day and to all other places of this creation bearing the scars of sin. Hold them dear and grant all that they need through Jesus Christ our Lord.

C Amen.

Offertory Prayer

A Let us pray. Holy Father,

C **We offer to you worship, praise, and thanks for all you have given. In response, take what we have given and use it for the entire creation, that we may join with you in the fight against sin, all evil and all harm. Through Jesus Christ our Lord. Amen.**

Proper Preface

P It is our duty and joy to give you thanks and praise. You stretch your arms wide and embrace the world that rejects you. Entrust in us the strength to be your witnesses just as those who have gone before have done, and welcome us at your feet as we join in the eternal hymn:

Communion Welcome

P   God's love is here, come and share in the good news.

Post Communion Blessing

P   May this gift of God's very self, in flesh and blood, give you courage to bear your own crosses.
C   **Amen.**

Post-Communion Prayer

A   Let us pray, Merciful God,
C   **We are weak and need your aid. Renew our spirit with this meal. Make it nourishment for the journeys that lie ahead, and may it draw us out to share with others the good news of your love. Amen.**

Benediction

P   May Christ who bears the heart of God instill in you the peace and strength to love and serve your neighbors with the love that God first showed us.
C   **Amen.**

Dismissal

A   Go forward with the cross as your guide.
C   **We follow the prince of peace. Amen!**

Maundy Thursday

Lenten Theme: Conversations With Jesus; The Last Supper

<u>Texts</u>
Exodus 12:1-4 (5-10) 11-14
Psalm 116:1-2, 12-19
1 Corinthians 11:23-26
John 13:1-17, 31b-35

Music Of The Day Traditional Hymns

"Eat This Bread, Drink This Cup" (ELW492, GG527, UMH628)
"Abide With Me" (ELW629, GG836, UMH700, H662)
"The King Of Love My Shepherd Is" (ELW502, GG802, UMH138, H645)
"One Bread One Body" (ELW496)
"Stay With Me" (ELW348, GG204)

Music Of The Day Contemporary Songs

"With All I Am" by Zschech (ccli.com SongSelect)
"Make Us One" by Paris (ccli.com SongSelect)
"How Beautiful" by Paris (dakotaroadmusic.com)
"One Hope" by Morgan/Zschech (ccli.com SongSelect)
"At The Cross" by Paris (ccli.com SongSelect)

Important Items

This is a great day to celebrate First Communion, as we have the story of the Last Supper.

Invocation

(omitted as a reflection of the continuation of the Ash Wednesday liturgy)

Forgiveness

(Tradition is that Maundy Thursday is the beginning of the end of what started on Ash Wednesday, as such, individual forgiveness is offered by inviting people forward to the chancel to receive a cross traced on their foreheads, this time without ashes.)

P   Come forward; your fasting has ended and you shall receive forgiveness for your repentance.

P   *(To the individuals that come forward)* your sins are forgiven in the name of the Father, Son, and Holy Spirit. *(Forgiveness can be accompanied by a hug.)*

Apostolic Greeting

P   May the love of Christ be yours this day and always.

C   **And also with you.**

Prayer Of The Day

A   Let us pray. Holy God,

C   **in the bread and wine, Jesus began a new relationship with humanity. In the washing of feet, your Son showed humility beyond comprehension. By these merciful acts bring us into a right relationship with you and with those around us through Jesus Christ, our Savior and Lord, who lives and reigns with you and the Holy Spirit, one God, now and forever. Amen.**

Washing Of The Hands

(Rather than the washing of the feet, this ceremony is used after the gospel reading and before the meditation, the following explanation can be placed in the bulletin or spoken.)

In the time of Jesus, the washing of feet was customary when coming in from the dusty roads into the house of a host for dinner. The washing of feet was done by servants and slaves and was regarded as an act of humility. In our modern world, it is customary to wash one's hands before partaking in a meal but most people do this for themselves. The act of washing someone else's hands continues to have the notion of humility for both the one washing and the one being washed. For those who desire it, you may come forward at this time to participate in this simple, yet sacred act.

Prayers Of The Church

A   Lord, it is your banquet to which we are invited, your world in which we live, and your gifts that you have given to us. We humbly ask you to be our guide on the road that winds and has no straight route. Shield us from the darkness, keep our hearts in your care, and help us to use our gifts to serve you. You are the voice of calm when all other voices of the world speak words of chaos. It is you we wish to hear. Speak answers into our life for the questions we pose, help us to see that first we must start at the foot of the cross, where we embrace your love. You speak into our lives the word of forgiveness, of healing, and of cleansing. Wash away our sins and all those of all who feel the weight on their shoulders. Draw together your people through our lives and the work of all your servants in the world. For our pains, for our burdens, and for our illnesses we ask comfort, Lord. Grant healing and recovery to all in need. Our cup overflows with your mercy and blessings, gracious God. May our cup continue to overflow and may it flow out to others who yearn with empty cups. Make our lives reflections of your love. May we rejoice in you always, in this place and in the world beyond. All these things we ask through your Son, our Savior, Jesus Christ.

C   **Amen.**

Offertory Prayer

A   Let us pray. Merciful Lord,

C   **as you have first given to us, now we give back to you. Inspire generosity in us each and every day that we may serve in humility and offer everything we are to your service for the sake of the world in Jesus Christ's name. Amen.**

Proper Preface

P It is our service to you, Lord God, to return with thanks and praise in worship. You offered your very self to us by becoming flesh and offering yourself as a sacrifice. For this, and all else you have done to provide life for the creation we praise your name and join with the saints in their unending hymn:

Communion Welcome

P Gather at our Lord's table and receive the blessings of God.

Post-Communion Blessing

P May Christ's body and blood be ever active in your life.

C **Amen.**

Post-Communion Prayer

A Let us pray. Lord Jesus,

C **in this meal you have given us strength and hope for the future. Use this moment to draw us closer to you and bind with you in the redemption of all you have made, in your holy name we pray. Amen.**

Stripping Of The Altar

This is done to a reading of Psalm 88, performed slowly by the lector. By reading the verses two at a time with a pause in between, there is space to remove nine distinct items from the chancel area. Other adjustments could be made if there aren't nine distinct items, but here is an example: 1) Paten (bread plate), 2) Chalice (wine cup), 3) Corporal (cloth under communion elements), 4) First altar candle, 5) Second altar candle, 6) Lectern parament, 7) Altar parament or cloth, 8) Pastor's stole, 9) Recess to the back with the cross. There is no concluding dismissal.

Good Friday

Lenten Theme: Conversations With Jesus – The Cross

Texts
Isaiah 52:13-53:12
Psalm 22
Hebrews 10:16-25 alt. (Hebrews 4:14-16; 5:7-9)
John 18:1-19:42

> *Theme Alternative Texts*
> *This liturgy has a set of texts that march through some of the traditional stations of the cross.*

Music Of The Day is included in the service order below, and it is all traditional hymn-based music rather than contemporary, as this style fits best with the somber tone of Good Friday.

Important Notes

This liturgy should be performed with three people, or more if your particular situation allows. First, a cross bearer, indicated by "L" in the plan; second, a torch bearer, who has no speaking parts; and third, a pastor who will provide the meditation and is indicated as "P" who reads the lessons and gives the sermon. The procession goes cross bearer, then torch bearer, then pastor. The pastor should kneel at each of the stations if able. The procession moves during the singing of hymns.

This liturgy supposes side aisles whether at the edge of the nave or with pews/chairs on either side. You will want to map out the positions beforehand to know how to move about the sanctuary. Movement occurs clockwise, and if you can imagine the rear of the sanctuary as 6:00 and the chancel or front as 12, the readings should occur at 6, 7:30, 9, 10:30, 12, 1:30, 3, 4:30, and wrap up back at 6.

There are indications for when the congregation is to stand and sit. These are easily omitted, but are intended to give a sense of work and trudging.

If possible, dim the lights a little after each station and leave the congregation with just enough light to leave at the end.

Chimes should be played each time the congregation says, "Save in the cross of Christ our Lord."

Opening Hymn "Go To Dark Gethsemane" v. 1 (ELW347, GG220, UMH290, H171)

Invocation

P In the name of the Father, and of the Son, and of the Holy Spirit. **C Amen.**

P Lord, have mercy upon us. **C Lord, have mercy upon us.**

P Christ, have mercy upon us. **C Christ, have mercy upon us.**

P Lord, have mercy upon us. **C Lord, have mercy upon us.**

P Lord Jesus, you carried our sins in your own body on the tree so that we might have life. May we and all who remember this day find new life in you now and in the world to come, where you live and reign with the Father and the Holy Spirit, now and forever. **C Amen.**

L God forbid that I should glory: **C Save in the cross of Christ our Lord.**

Station 1 Hymn "Go To Dark Gethsemane" v. 2 (ELW347, GG220, UMH290, H171)

L God forbid that I should glory: **C Save in the cross of Christ our Lord.**

Stand

Station 1 Reading Matthew 27:11-26

L God forbid that I should glory: **C Save in the cross of Christ our Lord.**

P Almighty Father, we ask you to look with mercy on your children, for whom our Lord Jesus Christ was willing to be betrayed and to be given over to the hands of sinners and to suffer death on the cross.

C Amen.

Sit

Station 2 Hymn "O Sacred Head, Now Wounded" v. 1 (ELW351, GG221, UMH286, H168)

L God forbid that I should glory: **C Save in the cross of Christ our Lord.**

Stand

Station 2 Reading John 19:1-15

L God forbid that I should glory: **C Save in the cross of Christ our Lord.**

P Almighty Father, you have given your only begotten Son to die for us, and to rise again for our justification. Grant us so to put away the leaven of malice and wickedness, that we may always serve you in pureness of life and truth, through the merits of Jesus Christ our Lord.

C Amen.

Sit

Station 3 Hymn "Ah, Holy Jesus" vv. 1, 2 (ELW349, GG218, UMH289, H158)

L God forbid that I should glory: **C Save in the cross of Christ our Lord.**

Stand

Station 3 Reading John 19:16-17

L God forbid that I should glory: **C Save in the cross of Christ our Lord.**

P Almighty Father, your most dear Son did not enter joy before he suffered pain, and entered not into glory before he was crucified: Mercifully grant that we, walking in the way of the cross, may find it none other than the way of life and peace. **C Amen.**

Sit

Station 4 Hymn "When I Survey The Wondrous Cross" v. 1 (ELW803, GG223, UMH298, H474)
L   God forbid that I should glory: **C Save in the cross of Christ our Lord.**
Stand

Station 4 Reading Luke 23:26
L   God forbid that I should glory: **C Save in the cross of Christ our Lord.**
P   Father, your blessed Son has overcome death for our salvation: mercifully grant that we who have his glorious passion in remembrance may take up our cross daily and follow him. **C Amen.**
Sit

Station 5 Hymn "When I Survey The Wondrous Cross" v. 4 (ELW803, GG223, UMH298, H474)
L   God forbid that I should glory: **C Save in the cross of Christ our Lord.**
Stand

Station 5 Reading Luke 23:27-31
L   God forbid that I should glory: **C Save in the cross of Christ our Lord.**
P   Almighty and everlasting God, you hate nothing you have created, and you forgive the sins of all those who are sorrowful. Create and make in us new and contrite hearts, that we, worthily lamenting our sins and acknowledging our wretchedness, may obtain you, the God of all mercy, perfect remission, and forgiveness of all sins. **C Amen.**
Sit

Sermon

Station 6 Hymn *Choir Anthem* "How Beautiful" *by Paris/Harlan*
L   God forbid that I should glory: **C Save in the cross of Christ our Lord.**
Stand

Station 6 Reading Mark 15:22-27
L   God forbid that I should glory: **C Save in the cross of Christ our Lord.**
P   Father, by the passion of your blessed Son, you made the instrument of a shameful death to be to us a means of life and grace. Grant us, so to glory in the cross of Christ, that we may gladly suffer shame and loss for the sake of Jesus Christ our Lord. **C Amen.**
Sit

Station 7 Hymn "In the Cross of Christ I Glory" v. 1 (ELW324, GG213, UMH295, H441)
L   God forbid that I should glory: **C Save in the cross of Christ our Lord.**
Stand

Station 7 Reading Luke 23:34-43
L   God forbid that I should glory: **C Save in the cross of Christ our Lord.**
P   Lord God, your blessed Son, our Savior, gave his back to the smiters and hid not his face from shame. Grant us grace to take joyfully the sufferings of the present time, in full assurance of the glory that shall be ours through Christ our Lord. **C Amen.**
Sit

Station 8 Hymn "Alas! And Did My Savior Bleed" v. 1 (ELW337, GG212, UMH294)
L   God forbid that I should glory: **C Save in the cross of Christ our Lord.**
Stand

Station 8 Reading Luke 23:44-49
L   God forbid that I should glory: **C Save in the cross of Christ our Lord.**
P   Father, for our redemption, you gave your only Son to the death of the cross, and by his glorious resurrection you have delivered us from the power of our enemies. Grant that we may so die daily to sin, that we may evermore live with him in the joy of his holy resurrection, through Jesus Christ, your Son, our Lord. **C Amen.**
Sit

Station 9 Hymn "O Sacred Head, Now Wounded" v. 3 (ELW351, GG221, UMH286, H168)
L   God forbid that I should glory: **C Save in the cross of Christ our Lord.**
Stand

Station 9 Reading Luke 23:50-56
L   God forbid that I should glory: **C Save in the cross of Christ our Lord.**
P   Grant Lord, that as we are baptized into the death of your blessed Son, our Savior Jesus Christ, so by continually mortifying our corrupt affections, we may be buried with him; and that through the grave, and the gate of death, we may pass to our own joyful resurrection.
C Amen.
P   Lord, remember us in your kingdom and hear us as we pray:

The Lord's Prayer
Our Father, who art in heaven, hallowed be thy name, thy kingdom come, thy will be done, on earth as it is in heaven. Give us this day our daily bread; and forgive us our trespasses, as we forgive those who trespass against us; and lead us not into temptation, but deliver us from evil. For thine is the kingdom, and the power, and the glory, forever and ever. Amen.

We leave the church in silence and in the darkness that shall fill the Lord's house until we celebrate his resurrection.

Season Of Easter

Easter is the day and season inspiring our faith. While you'll note that there is not the same novel creativity here compared with the Christmas season, here the emphasis is on passion and tradition. The liturgy is written in such a way to be enthusiastic in each of the proclamations, prayers, and blessings. The overall theme is "God Speaks" and preaching for both the day and season should be quite simple — and a topic is provided for each day. Children's messages could concern what these words mean to young people; sermons the same thing for adults. The whole season thus becomes listening to God's word and teaching its meaning. If done by focusing on the simple phrases, it becomes powerful and easily memorable for those listening.

The confession and forgiveness, per tradition, is omitted for the season of Easter. In its place there is a litany for a thanksgiving for resurrection. Also, please note that there is an option to celebrate either Easter 7 or Ascension on the last Sunday of Easter.

On the day of Pentecost, there should be a ceremony akin to the lighting of the candles on Christmas Eve. Reuse the ones that have already been used, it is a symbolic reminder both of the promise from God made at Jesus' birth and the continuing presence of God through the Holy Spirit. Singing the hymn (recommended first and last verses of "Spirit of Gentleness" for traditional and "Holy Spirit Reign Down" for contemporary) with candles lit will ignite the memory of the Christ child and the hope that now rests on the tongues of the faithful.

Resurrection Of Our Lord

Easter Theme: God Speaks — What Does God Still Have to Say?

Texts
Acts 10:34-43
Psalm 118:1-2, 14-24
Colossians 3:1-4
John 20:1-18

Music Of The Day Traditional Hymns

"Jesus Christ Is Risen Today" (ELW365, GG232, H207)
"Now All The Vault Of Heaven Resounds/Ye Watchers And Ye Holy Ones" (ELW367, UMH90)
"I Know That My Redeemer Lives/From All That Dwell Below The Skies" (ELW619, UMH101)
"Let All Things Now Living" (ELW881, GG37)
"The Strife Is O'er The Battle Done" (ELW366, GG236, UMH306, H208)

Music Of The Day Contemporary Songs

"God Is Alive" by Fee/Kirkland (ccli.com SongSelect)
"My Redeemer Lives" by Morgan (ccli.com SongSelect)
"Mighty To Save" by Morgan/Fielding (ccli.com SongSelect)
"Glorious Day" by Bleecker/Hall (ccli.com SongSelect)
"Amen (Because He Lives)" by Maher (ccli.com SongSelect)
"My Savior Lives" by Egan/Packiam (ccli.com SongSelect)

Important Items

Earth Day is April 22.

Invocation

P In the name of the + Father, and the Son, and the Holy Spirit, who lives and reigns forever, bringing life and light to all the earth.
C **Amen.**

Easter Proclamation

P The darkness will never win, for the light, the Christ, the Savior of the world has risen from the dead!
C **Alleluia!**
P Death's sting will hold no more sway over us for Jesus Christ has triumphed over the grave!

C **Christ is risen!**
P Sun, moon, stars lift up your voice. Sing out in praise that our God stands victorious!
C **Christ is risen indeed! Alleluia!**

Thanksgiving For Resurrection

P Renewed by the gift of the empty tomb, let us give thanks for God's mercy.
(Silence for reflection)
P You restore the soul of everything by the air and wind.
C **Breathe life into our lungs!**
P You soothe the parched tongue and refresh us by the water.
C **Wash us by the waters!**
P You have taken our sin away by your death and resurrection. In the name of the Holy Trinity, + Father, Son, and Holy Spirit, may you know the blessings of our God in every step of your life.
C **Amen.**

Apostolic Greeting

P The grace of our Lord Jesus Christ, the love of God, and the communion of the Holy Spirit be with you all.
C **And also with you.**

Prayer Of The Day

A Let us pray. Almighty God,
C **we have been swept away as you have conquered not only every burden we endure, but even death itself. As we marvel at your power and might, draw us into holy living that our very lives may be continuing sign of your good news shouted into the depths of earth through the death and resurrection of Jesus Christ our Savior. Amen.**

Prayers Of The Church

A Filled with new life, we pray for all the world and all in need.
(Silence for reflection)
(After each petition)
A Life-giving God,
C **preach your good news.**
(After final petition)
A As you have granted blessings even beyond what we know we need, continue to pour out your gifts to those we name today and all else you see that we need, for the sake of the one who died for us, Jesus Christ our Lord.
C **Amen.**

Offertory Prayer

A Let us pray. Holy Lord,

C **we could never say thank you enough for all you have done. But take what we offer back to you so that resurrection and hope may be felt by those outside of these walls. Bless these gifts through the one who gave himself for us, Jesus Christ our Savior. Amen.**

Proper Preface

P It is right, it is our calling to return thanks to you, holy Father, for the work you have done in bringing your salvation to a desperate creation. As you trample death underfoot, you lift us to new life in you, just as you have done with all the saints throughout the ages. Unite our voices with theirs as we sing their unending hymn: (Sanctus)

Communion Welcome

P This is Jesus Christ, broken and poured out for you. Eat and be filled.

Post-Communion Blessing

P May the body and blood of Jesus Christ our Savior fill you with life and light.

C **Amen.**

Post-Communion Prayer

A Let us pray. Precious redeemer,

C **we are nothing without your grace. You have given us everything. Teach us again of what love means by this meal and send us out to share that message with those who need love, in your holy name. Amen.**

Benediction

P Witnesses of God, your eyes have seen and your ears have heard the power of God to forgive the sins. Now go out with that same Spirit. Bind up the wounds of the brokenhearted. Bless the world with your kindness. Be the voice of hope, in the name of the + Father, and the Son, and the Holy Spirit.

C **Amen.**

Dismissal

A Go spread the good news!

C **We will love the world! Amen!**

Easter 2

Easter Theme: God Speaks — Peace Be With You

Texts
Acts 2:14a, 22-32
Psalm 16
1 Peter 1:3-9
John 20:19-31

Music Of The Day Traditional Hymns
"Joyful, Joyful, We Adore Thee" (ELW836, LBW551, GG611, UMH89, H376)
"The Day Of Resurrection" (ELW361, H210)
"Christ The Lord Is Risen Today" (ELW373)
"Thine Is The Glory/Thine Be The Glory" (ELW376, GG238, UMH308)
"O Savior Precious Savior/O Jesus I Have Promised" (ELW820, LBW514, GG724, UMH396)

Music Of The Day Contemporary Songs
"My Redeemer Lives" by Morgan (ccli.com SongSelect)
"Christ Is Risen" by Jeremy Riddle (ccli.com SongSelect)
"Jesus My Redeemer" by Tomlin/Carson/Ingram (ccli.com SongSelect)
"What A Savior" by Jones/Story (ccli.com SongSelect)
"My Savior Lives" by Egan/Packiam (ccli.com SongSelect)

Important Items
The festival for Saint Mark is April 27.

Invocation
P   In the name of the + Father, and the Son, and the Holy Spirit, who lives and reigns forever, bringing life and light to all the earth.
C   **Amen.**

Easter Proclamation
P   The darkness will never win, for the light, the Christ, the Savior of the world has risen from the dead!
C   **Alleluia!**
P   Death's sting will hold no more sway over us for Jesus Christ has triumphed over the grave!
C   **Christ is risen!**

P Sun, moon, stars lift up your voice. Sing out in praise that our God stands victorious!
C **Christ is risen indeed! Alleluia!**

Thanksgiving For Resurrection

P Renewed by the gift of the empty tomb, let us give thanks for God's mercy.

(silence for reflection)

P You restore the soul of everything by the air and wind.
C **Breathe life into our lungs!**
P You soothe the parched tongue and refresh us by the water.
C **Wash us by the waters!**
P You have taken our sin away by your death and resurrection. In the name of the Holy Trinity, + Father, Son, and Holy Spirit, may you know the blessings of our God in every step of your life.
C **Amen.**

Apostolic Greeting

P The grace of our Lord Jesus Christ, the love of God, and the communion of the Holy Spirit be with you all.
C **And also with you.**

Prayer Of The Day

A Let us pray. Faithful God,
C **give us the eyes to bear witness to your mercy. Even if we don't fully understand, speak to us in hope so we may tell the story of your light that you bring into the world, through your Son, our Savior and Lord, Jesus the Christ. Amen.**

Prayers Of The Church

A Filled with new life, we pray for all the world and all in need.

(silence for reflection)

(after each petition)

A Life-giving God,
C **preach your good news.**

(after final petition)

A As you have granted blessings even beyond what we know we need, continue to pour out your gifts to those we name today and all else you see that we need, for the sake of the one who died for us, Jesus Christ our Lord.
C **Amen.**

Offertory Prayer

A Let us pray. Holy Lord,
C **we could never say thank you enough for all you have done. But take what we offer back to you so that resurrection and hope may be felt by those outside of these walls. Bless these gifts through the one who gave himself for us, Jesus Christ our Savior. Amen.**

Proper Preface

P   It is right, it is our calling to return thanks to you, holy Father, for the work you have done in bringing your salvation to a desperate creation. As you trample death underfoot, you lift us to new life in you, just as you have done with all the saints throughout the ages. Unite our voices with theirs as we sing their unending hymn: (Sanctus)

Communion Welcome

P   This is Jesus Christ, broken and poured out for you. Eat and be filled.

Post-Communion Blessing

P   May the body and blood of Jesus Christ our Savior fill you with life and light.

C   **Amen.**

Post-Communion Prayer

A   Let us pray. Precious redeemer,

C   **we are nothing without your grace. You have given us everything. Now teach us again of what love means by this meal and send us out to share that message with those who need love, in your holy name. Amen.**

Benediction

P   Witnesses of God, your eyes have seen and your ears have heard the power of God to forgive the sins. Go out with that same Spirit. Bind up the wounds of the brokenhearted. Bless the world with your kindness. Be the voice of hope, in the name of the + Father, and the Son, and the Holy Spirit.

C   **Amen.**

Dismissal

A   Go spread the good news!

C   **We will love the world! Amen!**

Easter 3

Easter Theme: God Speaks — It Was Necessary For Christ To Suffer

Texts
Acts 2:14a, 36-41
Psalm 116:1-4, 12-19
1 Peter 1:17-23
Luke 24:13-35

Music Of The Day Traditional Hymns
"Alleluia! Jesus Is Risen" (ELW377, WOV674)
"Good Christian Friends, Rejoice And Sing" (ELW385, GG239, H205)
"Baptized In Water" (ELW456, GG482, H294)
"Let Us Break Bread Together" (ELW471, GG525, UMH618, H325)
"On Our Way Rejoicing" (ELW537)

Music Of The Day Contemporary Songs
"This Is Amazing Grace" by Wickham (ccli.com SongSelect)
"That's Why We Praise Him" by Walker (ccli.com SongSelect)
"I Am" by Crowder (ccli.com SongSelect)
"God So Loved" by Morgan (ccli.com SongSelect)
"My Savior Lives" by Egan/Packiam (ccli.com SongSelect)

Important Items
The Festival For Saint Philip and Saint James is May 1.
Cinco de Mayo is May 5.

Invocation
P   In the name of the + Father, and the Son, and the Holy Spirit, who lives and reigns forever, bringing life and light to all the earth.
C   **Amen.**

Easter Proclamation
P   The darkness will never win, for the light, the Christ, the Savior of the world has risen from the dead!
C   **Alleluia!**
P   Death's sting will hold no more sway over us for Jesus Christ has triumphed over the grave!

C **Christ is risen!**

P Sun, moon, stars lift up your voice. Sing out in praise that our God stands victorious!

C **Christ is risen indeed! Alleluia!**

Thanksgiving For Resurrection

P Renewed by the gift of the empty tomb, let us give thanks for God's mercy.

(Silence for reflection)

P you restore the soul of everything by the air and wind.

C **Breathe life into our lungs!**

P you soothe the parched tongue and refresh us by the water.

C **Wash us by the waters!**

P you have taken our sin away by your death and resurrection. In the name of the Holy Trinity, + Father, Son, and Holy Spirit, may you know the blessings of our God in every step of your life.

C **Amen.**

Apostolic Greeting

P The grace of our Lord Jesus Christ, the love of God, and the communion of the Holy Spirit be with you all.

C **And also with you.**

Prayer Of The Day

A Let us pray. Ever-present God,

C **with you near, we are never alone. Your words inspire us to love those whom the world calls unlovable, and your welcome makes us feel as though we are never lost. Speak your truth to us, that we may recognize your presence in everyone we meet. Amen.**

Prayers Of The Church

A Filled with new life, we pray for all the world and all in need.

(silence for reflection)

(after each petition)

A Life-giving God

C **preach your good news.**

(after final petition)

A As you have granted blessings even beyond what we know we need, continue to pour out your gifts to those we name today and all else you see that we need, for the sake of the one who died for us, Jesus Christ our Lord.

C **Amen.**

Offertory Prayer

A Let us pray. Holy Lord,

C **we could never say thank you enough for all you have done. But take what we offer back to you so that resurrection and hope may be felt by those outside of these walls. Bless these gifts through the one who gave himself for us, Jesus Christ our Savior. Amen.**

Proper Preface

P It is right, it is our calling to return thanks to you, holy Father, for the work you have done in bringing your salvation to a desperate creation. As you trample death underfoot, you lift us to new life in you, just as you have done with all the saints throughout the ages. Unite our voices with theirs as we sing their unending hymn: (Sanctus)

Communion Welcome

P This is Jesus Christ, broken and poured out for you. Eat and be filled.

Post-Communion Blessing

P May the body and blood of Jesus Christ our Savior fill you with life and light.

C **Amen.**

Post-Communion Prayer

A Let us pray. Precious redeemer,

C **we are nothing without your grace. You have given us everything. Teach us again of what love means by this meal and send us out to share that message with those who need love, in your holy name. Amen.**

Benediction

P Witnesses of God, your eyes have seen and your ears have heard the power of God to forgive the sins. Go out with that same Spirit. Bind up the wounds of the brokenhearted. Bless the world with your kindness. Be the voice of hope, in the name of the + Father, and the Son, and the Holy Spirit.

C **Amen.**

Dismissal

A Go spread the good news!

C **We will love the world! Amen!**

Easter 4

Easter Theme: God Speaks — I Am The Good Shepherd

Texts
Acts 2:42-47
Psalm 23
1 Peter 2:19-25
John 10:1-10

Music Of The Day Traditional Hymns
"Praise To The Lord, The Almighty" (ELW858, GG35, UMH139, H390)
"The King Of Love My Shepherd Is" (ELW502, GG802, UMH138, H645)
"Savior Like A Shepherd Lead Us" (ELW782, GG187, UMH381, H708)
"Shepherd Me, O God" (ELW780, GG473)
"What A Fellowship, What A Joy Divine" (ELW774, GG837, UMH133)

Music Of The Day Contemporary Songs
"Shout For Joy" by Baloche/Brewster/Ingram (ccli.com SongSelect)
"How Can I Keep From Singing?" by Tomlin/Redman/Cash (ccli.com SongSelect)
"Hold Me Close" by Paris (ccli.com SongSelect)
"My Savior, My God" by Shust/Greenwell (ccli.com SongSelect)
"My Savior Lives" by Egan/Packiam (ccli.com SongSelect)

Invocation
P   In the name of the + Father, and the Son, and the Holy Spirit, who lives and reigns forever, bringing life and light to all the earth.
C   **Amen.**

Easter Proclamation
P   The darkness will never win, for the light, the Christ, the Savior of the world has risen from the dead!
C   **Alleluia!**
P   Death's sting will hold no more sway over us for Jesus Christ has triumphed over the grave!
C   **Christ is risen!**
P   Sun, moon, stars lift up your voice. Sing out in praise that our God stands victorious!
C   **Christ is risen indeed! Alleluia!**

Thanksgiving For Resurrection

P Renewed by the gift of the empty tomb, let us give thanks for God's mercy.

(Silence for reflection)

P You restore the soul of everything by the air and wind.

C **Breathe life into our lungs!**

P You soothe the parched tongue and refresh us by the water.

C **Wash us by the waters!**

P You have taken our sin away by your death and resurrection. In the name of the Holy Trinity, + Father, Son, and Holy Spirit, may you know the blessings of our God in every step of your life.

C **Amen.**

Apostolic Greeting

P The grace of our Lord Jesus Christ, the love of God, and the communion of the Holy Spirit be with you all.

C **And also with you.**

Prayer Of The Day

A Let us pray. Holy shepherd,

C **we follow Your call for our lives. Speak to us words of challenge and guidance so that we can follow where You lead, and that we can know Your will. In your holy name we pray. Amen.**

Prayers Of The Church

A Filled with new life, we pray for all the world and all in need.

(Silence for reflection)

(After each petition)

A Life-giving God,

C **preach your good news.**

(After final petition)

A As you have granted blessings even beyond what we know we need, continue to pour out your gifts to those we name today and all else You see that we need, for the sake of the one who died for us, Jesus Christ our Lord.

C **Amen.**

Offertory Prayer

A Let us pray. Holy Lord,

C **we could never say thank you enough for all you have done. But take what we offer back to you so that resurrection and hope may be felt by those outside of these walls. Bless these gifts through the one who gave himself for us, Jesus Christ our Savior. Amen.**

Proper Preface

P It is right, it is our calling to return thanks to you, holy Father, for the work you have done in bringing your salvation to a desperate creation. As you trample death underfoot, you lift us to new life in you, just as you have done with all the saints throughout the ages. Unite our voices with theirs as we sing their unending hymn. (Sanctus)

Communion Welcome
P This is Jesus Christ, broken and poured out for you. Eat and be filled.

Post-Communion Blessing
P May the body and blood of Jesus Christ our Savior fill you with life and light.
C **Amen.**

Post-Communion Prayer
A Let us pray. Precious redeemer,
C **we are nothing without your grace. You have given us everything. Teach us again of what love means by this meal and send us out to share that message with those who need love, in your holy name. Amen.**

Benediction
P Witnesses of God, your eyes have seen and your ears have heard the power of God to forgive the sins. Go out with that same Spirit. Bind up the wounds of the brokenhearted. Bless the world with your kindness. Be the voice of hope, in the name of the + Father, and the Son, and the Holy Spirit.
C **Amen.**

Dismissal
A Go spread the good news!
C **We will love the world! Amen!**

Easter 5

Easter Theme: God Speaks — I Am The Way, The Truth, And The Life

Texts
Acts 7:55-60
Psalm 31:1-5, 15-16
1 Peter 2:2-10
John 14:1-14

Music Of The Day Traditional Hymns
"Christ Is Alive, Let Christians Sing" (ELW389, GG246, UMH318, H182)
"When We Are Living" (ELW639, GG822, UMH356,
"Be Thou My Vision" (ELW793, GG450, UMH451, H488)
"I Received The Living God" (ELW477)
"Alleluia, Alleluia, Give Thanks/Jesus Is Lord Of All The Earth" (WOV671, GG240, UMH162, H178)

Music Of The Day Contemporary Songs
"Everlasting God" by Brown/Riley (ccli.com SongSelect)
"Dwell In Your House" by Ewing (ccli.com SongSelect)
"10,000 Reasons" by Myrin/Redman (ccli.com SongSelect)
"The Words I Would Say" by McDonald/Frey/Mizell (ccli.com SongSelect)
"My Savior Lives" by Egan/Packiam (ccli.com SongSelect)

Important Items
The festival for Saint Matthias is May14.

Mothers' Day — forget at your own peril.

Armed Forces Day is May 20.

Invocation
P In the name of the + Father, and the Son, and the Holy Spirit, who lives and reigns forever, bringing life and light to all the earth.
C **Amen.**

Easter Proclamation

P   The darkness will never win, for the light, the Christ, the Savior of the world has risen from the dead!

C   Alleluia!

P   Death's sting will hold no more sway over us for Jesus Christ has triumphed over the grave!

C   Christ is risen!

P   Sun, moon, stars lift up your voice. Sing out in praise that our God stands victorious!

C   Christ is risen indeed! Alleluia!

Thanksgiving For Resurrection

P   Renewed by the gift of the empty tomb, let us give thanks for God's mercy.

(silence for reflection)

P   You restore the soul of everything by the air and wind.

C   Breathe life into our lungs!

P   You soothe the parched tongue and refresh us by the water.

C   Wash us by the waters!

P   You have taken our sin away by your death and resurrection. In the name of the Holy Trinity, + Father, Son, and Holy Spirit, may you know the blessings of our God in every step of your life.

C   Amen.

Apostolic Greeting

P   The grace of our Lord Jesus Christ, the love of God, and the communion of the Holy Spirit be with you all.

C   And also with you.

Prayer Of The Day

A   Let us pray. Holy truth,

C   there are times when we know you and times when we don't. There are times when we can see you clearly and times when we are blind. There are times when we listen, and others when we ignore. Continue to speak to us until our testimony is only and always of your goodness. Amen.

Prayers Of The Church

A   Filled with new life, we pray for all the world and all in need.

(Silence for reflection)

(After each petition)

A   Life-giving God,

C   preach your good news.

(After final petition)

A   As you have granted blessings even beyond what we know we need, continue to pour out your gifts to those we name today and all else you see that we need, for the sake of the one who died for us, Jesus Christ our Lord.

C   Amen.

Offertory Prayer

A Let us pray. Holy Lord,

C **we could never say thank you enough for all you have done. But take what we offer back to you so that resurrection and hope may be felt by those outside of these walls. Bless these gifts through the one who gave himself for us, Jesus Christ our Savior. Amen.**

Proper Preface

P It is right, it is our calling to return thanks to you, holy Father, for the work you have done in bringing your salvation to a desperate creation. As you trample death underfoot, you lift us to new life in you, just as you have done with all the Saints throughout the ages. Unite our voices with theirs as we sing their unending hymn: (Sanctus)

Communion Welcome

P This is Jesus Christ, broken and poured out for you. Eat and be filled.

Post-Communion Blessing

P May the body and blood of Jesus Christ our Savior fill you with life and light.

C **Amen.**

Post-Communion Prayer

A Let us pray. Precious redeemer,

C **we are nothing without your grace. You have given us everything. Teach us again of what love means by this meal and send us out to share that message with those who need love, in your holy name. Amen.**

Benediction

P Witnesses of God, your eyes have seen and your ears have heard the power of God to forgive the sins. Go out with that same Spirit. Bind up the wounds of the brokenhearted. Bless the world with your kindness. Be the voice of hope, in the name of the + Father, and the Son, and the Holy Spirit.

C **Amen.**

Dismissal

A Go spread the good news!

C **We will love the world! Amen!**

Easter 6

Easter Theme: God Speaks — I Will Come To You

Texts
Acts 17:22-31
Psalm 66:8-20
1 Peter 3:13-22
John 14:15-21

Music Of The Day Traditional Hymns
"Come Thou Almighty King" (ELW408, GG2, UMH61, H365)
"Children Of The Heavenly Father" (ELW781, UMH141)
"Many And Great, O God" (ELW837, WOV794, GG21, UMH148, H385)
"O Sing To The Lord" (ELW822, WOV795, GG637)
"Praise The Lord! O Heavens/Glorious Things Of Thee Are Spoken" (ELW823, GG81, UMH731, H522)

Music Of The Day Contemporary Songs
"Today Is The Day" by Brewster/Baloche (ccli.com SongSelect)
"Hallelujah" by Brown/Doerksen (ccli.com SongSelect)
"I Will Rise" by Giglio/Tomlin et al (ccli.com SongSelect)
"Sing Alleluia" by Hindalong/Byrd (ccli.com SongSelect)
"My Savior Lives" by Egan/Packiam (ccli.com SongSelect)

Invocation
P In the name of the + Father, and the Son, and the Holy Spirit, who lives and reigns forever, bringing life and light to all the earth.
C **Amen.**

Easter Proclamation
P The darkness will never win, for the light, the Christ, the Savior of the world has risen from the dead!
C **Alleluia!**
P Death's sting will hold no more sway over us for Jesus Christ has triumphed over the grave!
C **Christ is risen!**
P Sun, moon, stars lift up your voice. Sing out in praise that our God stands victorious!
C **Christ is risen indeed! Alleluia!**

Thanksgiving For Resurrection

P Renewed by the gift of the empty tomb, let us give thanks for God's mercy.

(silence for reflection)

P You restore the soul of everything by the air and wind.

C **Breathe life into our lungs!**

P You soothe the parched tongue and refresh us by the water.

C **Wash us by the waters!**

P You have taken our sin away by your death and resurrection. In the name of the Holy Trinity, + Father, Son, and Holy Spirit, may you know the blessings of our God in every step of your life.

C **Amen.**

Apostolic Greeting

P The grace of our Lord Jesus Christ, the love of God, and the communion of the Holy Spirit be with you all.

C **And also with you.**

Prayer Of The Day

A Let us pray. Merciful Creator,

C **you have aided us since the beginning of time. We need you in our lives each and every day. Continue to speak your words of comfort and peace to us so that we may be encouraged to be your disciples in our part of the world, through Jesus Christ our Lord. Amen.**

Prayers Of The Church

A Filled with new life, we pray for all the world and all in need.

(silence for reflection)

(after each petition)

A Life-giving God,

C **preach your good news.**

(after final petition)

A As you have granted blessings even beyond what we know we need, continue to pour out your gifts to those we name today and all else you see that we need, for the sake of the one who died for us, Jesus Christ our Lord.

C **Amen.**

Offertory Prayer

A Let us pray. Holy Lord,

C **we could never say thank you enough for all you have done. But take what we offer back to you so that resurrection and hope may be felt by those outside of these walls. Bless these gifts through the one who gave himself for us, Jesus Christ our Savior. Amen.**

Proper Preface

P It is right, it is our calling to return thanks to you, holy Father, for the work you have done in bringing your salvation to a desperate creation. As you trample death underfoot, you lift us to new life in you, just as you have done with all the Saints throughout the ages. Unite our voices with theirs as we sing their unending hymn: (Sanctus)

Communion Welcome

P This is Jesus Christ, broken and poured out for you. Eat and be filled.

Post-Communion Blessing

P May the body and blood of Jesus Christ our Savior fill you with life and light.

C **Amen.**

Post-Communion Prayer

A Let us pray. Precious redeemer,

C **we are nothing without your grace. You have given us everything. Teach us again of what love means by this meal and send us out to share that message with those who need love, in your holy name. Amen.**

Benediction

P Witnesses of God, your eyes have seen and your ears have heard the power of God to forgive the sins. Now go out with that same Spirit. Bind up the wounds of the brokenhearted. Bless the world with your kindness. Be the voice of hope, in the name of the + Father, and the Son, and the Holy Spirit.

C **Amen.**

Dismissal

A Go spread the good news!

C **We will love the world! Amen!**

Ascension Of Our Lord

Easter Theme: God Speaks — You Are Witnesses Of These Things

Texts
Acts 1:1-11
Psalm 47
Ephesians 1:15-23
Luke 24:44-53

Music Of The Day Traditional Hymns
"At The Name Of Jesus" (ELW416, LBW179, GG264, UMH168, H435)
"A Hymn Of Glory Let Us Sing" (ELW393, GG258)
"Beautiful Savior/Fairest Lord Jesus" (ELW838, GG630, H384)
"Jesus, Remember Me" (ELW616, GG227, UMH488)
"Give To Our God Immortal Praise" (ELW848, LBW520)

Music Of The Day Contemporary Songs
"Glory To God Forever" by Fee/Beeching (ccli.com SongSelect)
"Here I Am To Worship" by Hughes (ccli.com SongSelect)
"How Great Is Our God" by Tomlin/Reeves/Cash (ccli.com SongSelect)
"Agnus Dei" by Smith (ccli.com SongSelect)
"Jesus Messiah" by Carson/Tomlin et al (ccli.com SongSelect)

Important Items
Memorial Day.
The festival for the visitation of Mary to Elizabeth is May 31.

Invocation
P In the name of the + Father, and the Son, and the Holy Spirit, who lives and reigns forever, bringing life and light to all the earth.
C **Amen.**

Easter Proclamation
P The darkness will never win, for the light, the Christ, the Savior of the world has risen from the dead!
C **Alleluia!**
P Death's sting will hold no more sway over us for Jesus Christ has triumphed over the grave!

C **Christ is risen!**

P Sun, moon, stars lift up your voice. Sing out in praise that our God stands victorious!

C **Christ is risen indeed! Alleluia!**

Thanksgiving For Resurrection

P Renewed by the gift of the empty tomb, let us give thanks for God's mercy.

(Silence for reflection)

P You restore the soul of everything by the air and wind.

C **Breathe life into our lungs!**

P You soothe the parched tongue and refresh us by the water.

C **Wash us by the waters!**

P You have taken our sin away by your death and resurrection. In the name of the Holy Trinity, + Father, Son, and Holy Spirit, may you know the blessings of our God in every step of your life.

C **Amen.**

Apostolic Greeting

P The grace of our Lord Jesus Christ, the love of God, and the communion of the Holy Spirit be with you all.

C **And also with you.**

Prayer Of The Day

A Let us pray. Blessed God,

C **we feel the pain of your departure from Earth, as we could use you here and now more than ever. Yet, we trust that even though we can't see you, you are still with us. Speak with us the hope to continually worship and praise you even when we can't feel you near, through Jesus Christ our Lord. Amen.**

Prayers Of The Church

A Filled with new life, we pray for all the world and all in need.

(silence for reflection)

(after each petition)

A Life-giving God,

C **preach your good news.**

(after final petition)

A As you have granted blessings even beyond what we know we need, continue to pour out your gifts to those we name today and all else you see that we need, for the sake of the one who died for us, Jesus Christ our Lord.

C **Amen.**

Offertory Prayer

A Let us pray. Holy Lord,

C **we could never say thank you enough for all you have done. But take what we offer back to you so that resurrection and hope may be felt by those outside of these walls. Bless these gifts through the one who gave himself for us, Jesus Christ our Savior. Amen.**

Proper Preface

P   It is right, it is our calling to return thanks to you, holy Father, for the work you have done in bringing your salvation to a desperate creation. As you trample death underfoot, you lift us to new life in you, just as you have done with all the Saints throughout the ages. Unite our voices with theirs as we sing their unending hymn: (Sanctus)

Communion Welcome

P   This is Jesus Christ, broken and poured out for you. Eat and be filled.

Post-Communion Blessing

P   May the body and blood of Jesus Christ our Savior fill you with life and light.
C   **Amen.**

Post-Communion Prayer

A   Let us pray. Precious redeemer,
C   **we are nothing without your grace. You have given us everything. Teach us again of what love means by this meal and send us out to share that message with those who need love, in your holy name. Amen.**

Benediction

P   Witnesses of God, your eyes have seen and your ears have heard the power of God to forgive the sins. Go out with that same Spirit. Bind up the wounds of the brokenhearted. Bless the world with your kindness. Be the voice of hope, in the name of the + Father, and the Son, and the Holy Spirit.
C   **Amen.**

Dismissal

A   Go spread the good news!
C   **We will love the world! Amen!**

Easter 7

Easter Theme: God Speaks — Keep Them That They May Be One

Texts
Acts 1:6-14
Psalm 68:1-10, 32-35
1 Peter 4:12-14; 5:6-11
John 17:1-11

Music Of The Day Traditional Hymns
"Crown Him With Many Crowns" (ELW855, LBW170, GG268, UMH327, H494)
"Lord Of All Hopefulness" (ELW765, GG683, H482)
"Bind Us Together" (WOV748)
"You Are Mine/I Will Come To You In The Silence" (ELW581, GG177)
"The Church's One Foundation" (ELW654, GG321, UMH545, H525)

Music Of The Day Contemporary Songs
"Here To Eternity" by Zschech/Moyse (ccli.com SongSelect)
"Holy" by Brown (ccli.com SongSelect)
"I Could Sing Of Your Love Forever" by Smith (ccli.com SongSelect)
"Agnus Dei" by Smith (ccli.com SongSelect)
"My Savior Lives" by Egan/Packiam (ccli.com SongSelect)

Important Items
Memorial Day.

The festival for the visitation of Mary to Elizabeth is May 31.

Invocation
P   In the name of the + Father, and the Son, and the Holy Spirit, who lives and reigns forever, bringing life and light to all the earth.
C   **Amen.**

Easter Proclamation
P   The darkness will never win, for the light, the Christ, the Savior of the world has risen from the dead!
C   **Alleluia!**
P   Death's sting will hold no more sway over us for Jesus Christ has triumphed over the grave!

C **Christ is risen!**
P Sun, moon, stars lift up your voice. Sing out in praise that our God stands victorious!
C **Christ is risen indeed! Alleluia!**

Thanksgiving For Resurrection

P Renewed by the gift of the empty tomb, let us give thanks for God's mercy.
(Silence for reflection)
P You restore the soul of everything by the air and wind.
C **Breathe life into our lungs!**
P You soothe the parched tongue and refresh us by the water.
C **Wash us by the waters!**
P You have taken our sin away by your death and resurrection. In the name of the Holy Trinity, + Father, Son, and Holy Spirit, may you know the blessings of our God in every step of your life.
C **Amen.**

Apostolic Greeting

P The grace of our Lord Jesus Christ, the love of God, and the communion of the Holy Spirit be with you all.
C **And also with you.**

Prayer Of The Day

A Let us pray. Gracious king,
C **you do not abandon us to our own devices, but intercede on our behalf. We belong to you because you claimed us, and prayed for us and saved us. May our whole lives reflect your graciousness to us, and continue to speak on our behalf through Jesus Christ our Lord. Amen.**

Prayers Of The Church

A Filled with new life, we pray for all the world and all in need.
(silence for reflection)
(after each petition)
A Life-giving God,
C **preach your good news.**
(after final petition)
A As you have granted blessings even beyond what we know we need, continue to pour out your gifts to those we name today and all else you see that we need, for the sake of the one who died for us, Jesus Christ our Lord.
C **Amen.**

Offertory Prayer

A Let us pray. Holy Lord,
C **we could never say thank you enough for all you have done. But take what we offer back to you so**

that resurrection and hope may be felt by those outside of these walls. Bless these gifts through the one who gave himself for us, Jesus Christ our Savior. Amen.

Proper Preface

P   It is right, it is our calling to return thanks to you, holy Father, for the work you have done in bringing your salvation to a desperate creation. As you trample death underfoot, you lift us to new life in you, just as you have done with all the saints throughout the ages. Unite our voices with theirs as we sing their unending hymn: (Sanctus)

Communion Welcome

P   This is Jesus Christ, broken and poured out for you. Eat and be filled.

Post-Communion Blessing

P   May the body and blood of Jesus Christ our Savior fill you with life and light.
C   Amen.

Post-Communion Prayer

A   Let us pray. Precious redeemer,
C   we are nothing without your grace. You have given us everything. Now teach us again of what love means by this meal and send us out to share that message with those who need love, in your holy name. Amen.

Benediction

P   Witnesses of God, your eyes have seen and your ears have heard the power of God to forgive the sins. Go out with that same Spirit. Bind up the wounds of the brokenhearted. Bless the world with your kindness. Be the voice of hope, in the name of the + Father, and the Son, and the Holy Spirit.
C   Amen.

Dismissal

A   Go spread the good news!
C   We will love the world! Amen!

Day Of Pentecost

Easter Theme: God Speaks — And The Spirit Is Given

Texts
Acts 2:1-21
Psalm 104:24-34, 35b
1 Corinthians 12:3b-13
John 20:19-23

Music Of The Day Traditional Hymns
"Come, Thou Fount Of Every Blessing" (ELW807, GG475, UMH400, H686)
"Lord Let My Heart Be Good Soil" (ELW512)
"Spirit Of Gentleness" (ELW396, WOV684)
"Spirit Of God, Descend Upon My Heart" (ELW800, GG688, UMH500)
"Go My Children With My Blessing/God That Madest Earth And Heaven" (ELW543, GG547, UMH688)

Music Of The Day Contemporary Songs
"All Over The World" by Redman/Smith (ccli.com SongSelect)
"Holy Is The Lord" by Tomlin/Giglio (ccli.com SongSelect)
"Holy Spirit" by Torwalt (ccli.com SongSelect)
"Holy Spirit Rain Down" by Fragar (ccli.com SongSelect)
"Build Your Kingdom Here" by Rend Collective Experiment (ccli.com SongSelect)

Invocation
P   Blessed be the name of our God: Father, Son, and Holy Spirit who inspires us to hope and faith.
C   **Amen.**

Thanksgiving For Resurrection
P   Renewed by the gift of the empty tomb, let us give thanks for God's mercy.
(Silence for reflection)
P   You restore the soul of everything by the air and wind.
C   **Breathe life into our lungs!**
P   You soothe the parched tongue and refresh us by the water.
C   **Wash us by the waters!**
P   You have taken our sin away by your death and resurrection. In the name of the Holy Trinity, + Father, Son, and Holy Spirit, may you know the blessings of our God in every step of your life.
C   **Amen.**

Apostolic Greeting

P The Spirit of gentleness and peace be with you this day.

C **And also with you.**

Prayer Of The Day

A Let us pray. Abiding Savior,

C **you have breathed the life-giving Spirit into our lungs, calling us from death to life, and gifting us for every good work. Live and move in us that all we say and do will be seen as a sign of your glory alive in the world. Amen.**

Prayers Of The Church

A Sent forth by the Spirit, let us relieve the burdens of the creation by asking for God's mercy.

(silence for reflection)

Begin each petition with a gift of the Spirit

Spirit of wisdom

Spirit of faith

Spirit of healing

Spirit of prophecy

Spirit of discernment

(after each petition)

A Hear us as we pray,

C **and bless us by your gifts.**

(after final petition)

A We offer all this and anything else that you see we need to you, and trust in your faithfulness to us through Jesus Christ our Lord.

C **Amen.**

Offertory Prayer

A Let us pray. O God,

C **you pour your gifts into every generation. We have been given an abundance and return to you what you have first given us. By your Holy Spirit, continue to send us out to do the work of your kingdom and return to you in generosity, through Jesus Christ our Savior. Amen.**

Proper Preface

P It is only with the help of the Spirit that our voice cries out in joy to you, Lord of our lives. You have given us all things, and to sustain us through the joys and sorrows, you have poured out yourself into us through the Holy Spirit. With this breath in our lungs, we sing out in joy to you with the saints of the entire body of Christ: (Sanctus)

Communion Welcome

P Come and be strengthened by the body and blood of our Savior.

Post-Communion Blessing

P May the bread and wine give life to your body that you may be a gift of life to your neighbor.

C Amen.

Post-Communion Prayer

A Let us pray. Holy Spirit,

C do not leave our side. As we go out to worship God by loving and serving the creation, give us the words to speak, and the confidence from this meal of love, to reach out to all who need the good news of Jesus Christ. Amen.

Candlelighting Litany

P The Spirit is poured out into you.

C We are the light of the world.

P The Spirit gives gifts to each.

C We are the salt of the earth.

P The Spirit gives life to all.

C May we see visions of what creation could be.

(sing song with candles lit)

Benediction

P May the light of Christ be alive in you, each and every day.

C Amen.

Dismissal

A Go in peace, renewed by the Spirit.

C Thanks be to God. Amen!

Season After Pentecost

This season is another "green" season in the church year, symbolizing growth and life. It covers nearly half of the year from its beginning to its end and it is suggested to be broken into two distinct parts: June — August and September — November. Its themes are "planting" and "harvesting" respectively. It does not really coincide with the harvest season as it currently exists, but rather is intended to be a division for how to develop a sense of development in worship. Each month has a completely rewritten liturgy (not including festivals that have their own). Also, please note there is an option in 2017 for celebrating Reformation Sunday or Proper 24 on October 30, though since this is the 500th anniversary of the Reformation that festival is preferred.

During "planting" season, two things should be gathered: a list of favorite Bible verses/stories and a list of favorite hymns. Simple forms can be distributed in the narthex or bulletin to input the requests. Yes, those forms should also request people's names, not necessarily for publicity (though it could be interesting to post in the bulletin whose favorite verse was being read that day), but for pastoral interest. If these are people to whom you are called to minister, what better way than to ask them about their spirituality in light of their favorite Bible verse or hymn?

During "harvest" season, these collected items are put to use. The hymns are quite obvious, that you would use the hymns that people selected throughout the season. The Bible verses are a little bit different. If someone is vulnerable enough to offer interest, something should be done about it. Two suggestions for how to handle this: One, as a start to the liturgy invite people to bring their own personal Bibles and read and highlight those verses that are meaningful to the people with whom they worship, building community. Two, create a sermon and a liturgy (or at least a Prayer Of The Day) in the image of a Bible verse or story, replacing one of the Sundays in the season (preferably not festival Sundays). This does create a bit more work, but since it is a given that some people will pick John 3:16 and Psalm 23 for their verses, a few examples will be given after the final full liturgy. Note that all readings for a given Sunday do not necessarily need to be replaced. If planning to still follow the lectionary closely, the gospel narrative should remain and the custom verses should be used in place of the New Testament reading for the day. Hopefully this will help people spend a bit more time with their Bibles than they are accustomed to doing and will help grow a sense of community as well.

One additional note, there is a specific proposal for the reading of names during the All Saints Sunday worship that needs some explanation. It is recommended that five candles be placed in the shape of the cross (symbolizing the five wounds of Christ) in some fashion so that people can see it. We used a wooden cross at the front of the chancel filled with sand and set the five candles in the sand. Depending on resources and chancel layout that may not be possible. However, the closer the people can get to the candles during communion, the better as it creates a powerful experience. As to the actual ceremony, in preparation, the list of names of the saints should be divided in four close-to-equal parts. At the beginning, a verse should be sung, then the brief prayer read, then the first candle lit. As the candle is lit, if it's possible to have chimes sound close to the moment the candle is lit, it is a nice addition. Then the first quarter of the names are read, slowly. The second candle is lit, with chimes. This pattern continues until the end when the brief prayer is read and the verse is sung concluding the ceremony.

Holy Trinity

Season After Pentecost Theme: Planting

Texts
Genesis 1:1-2:4a
Psalm 8
2 Corinthians 13:11-13
Matthew 28:16-20

Music Of The Day Traditional Hymns

"Holy, Holy, Holy" (ELW413, GG592, UMH64, H362)
"Lord Let My Heart Be Good Soil" (ELW512; ccli.com SongSelect)
"All Creatures Of Our God And King" (LBW527, GG15, UMH62, H400)
"Holy God, We Praise Your Name" (ELW414, GG4, UMH79, H366)
"Give To Our God Immortal Praise/From All That Dwell Below The Skies" (ELW848, UMH101)

Music Of The Day Contemporary Songs

"Father, Spirit, Jesus" by Hall/Cates/Hunt (ccli.com SongSelect)
"Indescribable" by Laura Story (ccli.com SongSelect)
"Holy, Holy, Holy" arr. by Morgan (ccli.com SongSelect)
"Breathe" by Marie Barnett (ccli.com SongSelect)
"How Majestic" by Jobe/Tomlin et al (ccli.com SongSelect)

Important Items

The festival for Saint Barnabas is today.

Flag Day is June 14.

Invocation

P   We begin in the name of the one who is, who was, and who is to come, who calls us forth from chaos to new life.

C   **Amen.**

Confession And Forgiveness

P   Standing before God and our brothers and sisters, let us offer our plea to God for forgiveness.
(Silence for reflection)

P Almighty Lord,

C the entire creation was laid out before us, and we took it to be our own, rather than to tend it as you commanded. We have been selfish, greedy, and dismissive in all of our actions. Wash away our sins from us, and bring us into new life in Jesus Christ our Savior. Amen.

P God has chosen us as children, even though we didn't deserve it. In the majestic name of + Christ, all your sins are taken away, that you may be disciples.

C Amen.

Apostolic Greeting

P May the God of love and peace be with you always.

C And also with you.

Prayer Of The Day

A Let us pray. Eternal king,

C you created the beginning and you hold the end. Teach us what we need to know, and help us to have faith for what we cannot understand. Help us to be your people, marvelous one in three and three in one. Amen.

(Traditionally the Athanasian Creed is recited on this day.)

Prayers Of The Church

A Called to be a part of the Holy Trinity, let us bring petitions for all those who are in need
(Silence for reflection)
(After each petition)
A God of love,

C hear us as we pray.
(After final petition)
A All things belong to you, heavenly Trinity. Enliven us by your breath and speak into creation all that we need this day, through your infinite mercy shown through Jesus Christ our Lord.

C Amen.

Offertory Prayer

A Let us pray. Creator God,

C you have placed into our hands the birds, the animals, the plants and all things and called them good. As we return these gifts to you, continue to make them sacred for the sake of bringing life to the whole world in Jesus' name. Amen.

Proper Preface

P It is right that we praise you holy three in one and one in three for your continued acts of creation, love, and life. You spoke all things into creation, and we speak back to you in joy for the work your hands have made. Joining together with all of the saints, we sing the eternal hymn of praise to you:

Communion Welcome

P God has given this bread and wine for you. Come and gather at the table.

Post-Communion Blessing

P May the body and blood of Jesus our Lord grant us the grace and mercy to live in peace with the world.

C **Amen.**

Post-Communion Prayer

A Let us pray. Merciful God,

C **you have given us food and drink for our souls. As you reach out to join with us in our lives, strengthen us by this bread and wine and remind us always of the sacrifice that came with it, that of Jesus Christ our Lord. Amen.**

Benediction

P May God, + Father, Son, and Holy Spirit dance with you in creation, bringing life to all you touch.

C **Amen.**

Dismissal

A Go and make disciples everywhere, for Christ is with you.

C **Amen!**

Proper 6 / Ordinary Time 11

Season After Pentecost Theme: Planting

Texts
Genesis 18: 1-15 (21:1-7)
Psalm 116:1-2, 12-19
Romans 5:1-8
Matthew 9:35-10:8 (9-23)

Music Of The Day Traditional Hymns
"Lift High The Cross/Come Christians Follow" (ELW660, GG826, UMH159)
"Lord Let My Heart Be Good Soil" (ELW512; ccli.com SongSelect)
"My Hope Is Built On Nothing Less" (ELW597, GG353, UMH368)
"Father Most Holy/Father We Praise Thee" (ELW415, UMH680, H1)
"This Is My Father's World" (ELW824, GG370, UMH144, H651)

Music Of The Day Contemporary Songs
"God Of Wonders" by Byrd/Hindalong (ccli.com SongSelect)
"Blessed Be Your Name" by Matt Redman (ccli.com SongSelect)
"Cornerstone" by Myrin/Morgan (ccli.com SongSelect)
"Worn" by Ingram/Donehey/Owen (ccli.com SongSelect)
"Shout To the Lord" by Zschech (ccli.com SongSelect)

Important Items
Today is Father's Day. A petition in the prayers should be used in thanksgiving for fathers.

The Festival of the Nativity of Saint John the Baptist is on June 24.

Invocation
P Blessed be the + Lord our God for whom no thing is too wonderful, who returns to us bearing fruit in due season.
C **Amen.**

Confession And Forgiveness
P Let us, in response to God's goodness, confess our sins.
(Pause for reflection)
P Merciful Lord,

C we have not held true to our promises and commitments. We have failed to love those you asked us to love with the sacrificial love you first showed us. Our trust needs your support. Open your arms to us that we may again call you Lord. Amen.

P As almighty God has cared for the birds of the air, and even more God cares for you. Through the blood of + Christ your sins are forgiven now and always. Amen.

Apostolic Greeting

P May Christ be your home and peace this day and always.

C Amen.

Prayer Of The Day

A Let us pray. Holy Father,

C you call us each by name in service to your word. Teach us to bring the good news of your kingdom to those who are lost. Give us courage to face the trials along the way so that we may join with you in bringing a fruitful harvest. Amen.

Prayers Of The Church

A Let us build up our community by praying for those in need.

(Silence for reflection)

(After each petition)

A Through the gift of Christ,

C bring darkness to light.

(After last petition)

A By your covenant throughout the generations, we entrust to you all for whom we pray this day through Jesus Christ our Lord.

C Amen.

Offertory Prayer

A Let us pray. Blessed God,

C your grace is poured out from age to age. We thank you for giving us what we need for the sake of our mission. Now, as we return our gifts to you, may you continue your mission in the hearts and minds of those still in need. We pray this through Jesus Christ who gave his life for us. Amen.

Proper Preface

P It is right that we always give thanks and praise to God who plants and harvests gifts and blessings to the world. Through Christ, who died so that sin may have no more power, we rejoice that we have been raised to new life with God. In thanksgiving for the grace given to us, we join together with the saints of heaven and earth in the unending hymn:

Communion Welcome

P   Christ asks you to come and eat the fruits of his work. Come and be fed.

Post-Communion Blessing

P   May the body and blood of our Lord Jesus Christ produce character and hope in you as you go forth into the world.

C   **Amen.**

Post-Communion Prayer

A   Let us pray. Life-giving Savior,

C   **you give us nourishment for the work we must do. By this bread and wine that you give for our sake, turn our minds and hearts to regard all we encounter with the same love you show for us. Amen.**

Benediction

P   May your trials produce endurance, may your endurance produce character and may your character produce hope for the days ahead. In the name of the + Father, Son, and Holy Spirit.

C   **Amen.**

Dismissal

A   Go out in peace to serve the world with kindness.

C   **In Jesus' name, Amen!**

Proper 7 / Ordinary Time 12

Season After Pentecost Theme: Planting

Texts
Genesis 21:8-21
Psalm 86:1-10, 16-17
Romans 6:1b-11
Matthew 10:24-39

Music Of The Day Traditional Hymns
"Let The Whole Creation Cry" (ELW876, GG679)
"Lord Let My Heart Be Good Soil" (ELW512; ccli.com SongSelect)
"Amazing Grace" (ELW779, GG649, UMH378, H671)
"I Was There To Hear Your Borning Cry" (ELW732, GG488)
"Let All Things Now Living" (ELW881, LBW557, GG37)

Music Of The Day Contemporary Songs
"Forever" by Tomlin (ccli.com SongSelect)
"The Only Name (Yours Will Be)" by Cowart (ccli.com SongSelect)
"Amazing Grace (My Chains Are Gone)" by Newton/Tomlin et al (ccli.com SongSelect)
"My Hope" by Zschech (ccli.com SongSelect)
"Amen" by Fitts (ccli.com SongSelect)

Important Items
The festival day for Saint Peter and Saint Paul is June 29.

Invocation
P Blessed be the + Lord our God for whom no thing is too wonderful, who returns to us bearing fruit in due season.
C **Amen.**

Confession And Forgiveness
P Let us, in response to God's goodness, confess our sins.
(Pause for reflection)
P Merciful Lord,
C **we have not held true to our promises and commitments. We have failed to love those you asked us**

to love with the sacrificial love you first showed us. Our trust needs your support. Open your arms to us that we may again call you Lord. Amen.

P As almighty God has cared for the birds of the air, and even more God cares for you. Through the blood of + Christ your sins are forgiven now and always. Amen.

Apostolic Greeting

P May Christ be your home and peace this day and always.

C **Amen.**

Prayer Of The Day

A Let us pray. Lord of all,

C **take away our fear. Help us to trust in your sustenance in the face of a world turned upside down, and to give thanks for the ways you give us life in the wilderness, through Jesus Christ our Lord. Amen.**

Prayers of the Church

A Let us build up our community by praying for those in need.

(Silence for reflection)

(After each petition)

A Through the gift of Christ,

C **bring darkness to light.**

(After last petition)

A By your covenant throughout the generations, we entrust to you all for whom we pray this day through Jesus Christ our Lord.

C **Amen.**

Offertory Prayer

A Let us pray. Blessed God,

C **your grace is poured out from age to age. We thank you for giving us what we need for the sake of our mission. Now, as we return our gifts to you, may you continue your mission in the hearts and minds of those still in need. We pray this through Jesus Christ who gave his life for us. Amen.**

Proper Preface

P It is right that we always give thanks and praise to God who plants and harvests gifts and blessings to the world. Through Christ, who died so that sin may have no more power, we rejoice that we have been raised to new life with God. In thanksgiving for the grace given to us, we join together with the saints of heaven and earth in the unending hymn: (Sanctus)

Communion Welcome

P Christ asks you to come and eat the fruits of his work. Come and be fed.

Post-Communion Blessing

P   May the body and blood of our Lord Jesus Christ produce character and hope in you as you go forth into the world.

C   **Amen.**

Post-Communion Prayer

A   Let us pray. Life-giving Savior,

C   **you give us nourishment for the work we must do. By this bread and wine which you give for our sake, turn our minds and hearts to regard all we encounter with the same love you show for us. Amen.**

Benediction

P   May your trials produce endurance, may your endurance produce character and may your character produce hope for the days ahead. In the name of the + Father, Son, and Holy Spirit.

C   **Amen.**

Dismissal

A   Go out in peace to serve the world with kindness.

C   **In Jesus' name, Amen!**

Proper 8 / Ordinary Time 13

Season After Pentecost Theme: Planting

Texts
Genesis 22:1-14
Psalm 13
Romans 6:12-23
Matthew 10:40-42

Music Of The Day Traditional Hymns
"O Beautiful For Spacious Skies" (ELW888, GG338, UMH696, H719)
"Lord Let My Heart Be Good Soil" (ELW512; ccli.com SongSelect)
"For The Beauty of the Earth" (ELW879, GG14, UMH92, H416)
"Just As I Am Without One Plea" (ELW592, LBW296, GG442, UMH357, H693)
"Mine Eyes Have Seen The Glory" (ELW890, GG354, UMH717)

Music Of The Day Contemporary Songs
"Free To Dance" by Zschech (ccli.com SongSelect)
"O Beautiful For Spacious Skies" (ccli.com SongSelect)
"Amazing Grace" (ccli.com SongSelect)
"The Power Of Your Love" by Bullock (ccli.com SongSelect)
"All The People Said Amen" by Maher/Morgan/Moak (ccli.com SongSelect)

Important Items
The holiday celebrating American independence is July 4, a prayer petition should be reserved affirming freedom.

The festival for Saint Thomas is July 3.

Invocation
P   Come and bless us by your presence, + Father, Son, and Holy Spirit and plant good seed into our hearts.
C   Amen.

Confession And Forgiveness
P   Let us approach God, confessing how we are slaves to sin.
(Pause for reflection)

P   Merciful Father,

C   **we do not know how to pray as we should. We do not act the ways we want, but do the very evil we don't want. Help us to live according to the Spirit rather than flesh, and take our sin away from us, that we may again bear witness that we are children of God. Amen.**

P   Indeed, you are called by the Spirit to be children of God, and by the passion of + Christ you are washed and made new. Together we cry out in thanksgiving.

C   **Abba, Father! Thank you. Amen!**

Apostolic Greeting

P   Inheritors of God's goodness, grace and peace be with you,

C   **and also with you.**

Prayer Of The Day

A   Let us pray. God our shelter,

C   **help us to trust in your goodness. May we recognize the little ones in need and offer them a cup of water and anything else that they need so we may again welcome you into our lives. Amen.**

Prayers Of The Church

A   We call out to God in prayer on behalf of those who face all manner of persecution and hardship.

(Pause for reflection)

(After each petition)

A   Come to us, Christ,

C   **and relieve our burdens.**

(If there is a celebratory prayer, use the following instead)

A   Give voice to our joy.

C   **Thanks be to God.**

(After the final petition)

A   By your Spirit, intercede on behalf of those in need with sighs too deep for words.

C   **Amen.**

Offertory Prayer

A   Let us pray. Gracious God,

C   **the gifts you have planted have grown. Now gather these gifts to yourself and grow the kingdom from a small seed into a large tree, and comfort all in the branches of its shelter, through Jesus Christ our Lord. Amen.**

Proper Preface

P   It is indeed our task and celebration to give thanks and praise to you, who pours out the seed, who gives growth in season and who gathers into your kingdom. With those who have been caught and gathered through the ages, we join together in the unending hymn of praise:

Communion Welcome

P It is time to be gathered and eat together as a family in Christ.

Post-Communion Blessing

P May the body and blood of Jesus Christ be a great pearl for your week, a moment of great excitement, and a sign of the kingdom borne out in you.

C **Amen.**

Post-Communion Prayer

A Let us pray. Life-giving Creator,

C **with thanks we take what you have given to us, your very flesh, and we feel your presence still with us. Help us to join together as one in this meal and to bring others to your feast, through our savior Jesus Christ. Amen.**

Benediction

P You have been given words of life. Go, in the + name of Jesus Christ and carry the living word to the corners of the earth.

C **Amen.**

Dismissal

A Follow the light on your path,

C **with the word as our guide. Amen!**

Proper 9 / Ordinary Time 14

Season After Pentecost Theme: Planting

Texts
Genesis 24:34-38, 42-49, 58-67
Psalm 45:10-17
Romans 7:15-25a
Matthew 11:16-19, 25-30

Music Of The Day Traditional Hymns

"Gather Us In/Here In This Place" (ELW532, GG401)
"Lord Let My Heart Be Good Soil" (ELW512; ccli.com SongSelect)
"O Word Of God Incarnate" (ELW514, GG459, UMH598)
"Softly And Tenderly Jesus Is Calling" (ELW608, GG418, UMH348)
"For The Fruit Of All Creation" (ELW679, GG36, UMH97b, H424)

Music Of The Day Contemporary Songs

"Thrive" by West/Hall (ccli.com SongSelect)
"The Lord Our God" by Stanfill/Ingram (ccli.com SongSelect)
"How Great Is Our God" by Tomlin/Reeves/Cash (ccli.com SongSelect)
"Thy Word" by Smith (ccli.com SongSelect)
"Let The Peace Of God Reign" by Zschech (ccli.com SongSelect)

Invocation

P   Come and bless us by your presence, + Father, Son, and Holy Spirit and plant good seed into our hearts.
C   **Amen.**

Confession And Forgiveness

P   Let us approach God, confessing how we are slaves to sin.
(Pause for reflection)
P   Merciful Father,
C   **we do not know how to pray as we should. We do not act the ways we want, but do the very evil we don't want. Help us to live according to the Spirit rather than flesh, and take our sin away from us, that we may again bear witness that we are children of God. Amen.**
P   Indeed, you are called by the Spirit to be children of God, and by the passion of + Christ you are washed and made new. Together we cry out in thanksgiving.
C   **Abba, Father! Thank you. Amen!**

Apostolic Greeting

P Inheritors of God's goodness, grace and peace be with you.

C And also with you.

Prayer Of The Day

A Let us pray. God our strength,

C help ease the burdens of our days. Open our eyes to the blessings of the world all around us and call us to give thanks and praise at the wonders of your hand, through our Lord and Savior Jesus Christ. Amen.

Prayers Of The Church

A We call out to God in prayer on behalf of those who face all manner of persecution and hardship.

(Pause for reflection)

(After each petition)

A Come to us, Christ,

C and relieve our burdens.

(If there is a celebratory prayer, use the following instead)

A Give voice to our joy.

C Thanks be to God.

(After the final petition)

A By your Spirit, intercede on behalf of those in need with sighs too deep for words.

C Amen.

Offertory Prayer

A Let us pray. Gracious God,

C the gifts You have planted have grown. Now gather these gifts to yourself and grow the kingdom from a small seed into a large tree, and comfort all in the branches of its shelter, through Jesus Christ our Lord. Amen. (Sanctus)

Proper Preface

P It is indeed our task and celebration to give thanks and praise to you, who pours out the seed, who gives growth in season and who gathers into your kingdom. With those who have been caught and gathered through the ages, we join together in the unending hymn of praise:

Communion Welcome

P It is time to be gathered and eat together as a family in Christ

Post-Communion Blessing

P May the body and blood of Jesus Christ be a great pearl for your week, a moment of great excitement, and a sign of the kingdom borne out in you.

C Amen.

Post-Communion Prayer

A Let us pray. Life-giving Creator,

C **with thanks we take what you have given to us, your very flesh, and we feel your presence still with us. Help us to join together as one in this meal and to bring others to your feast, through our Savior Jesus Christ. Amen.**

Benediction

P You have been given words of life. Go, in the + name of Jesus Christ and carry the living word to the corners of the earth.

C **Amen.**

Dismissal

A Follow the light on your path

C **with the word as our guide. Amen!**

Proper 10 / Ordinary Time 15

Season After Pentecost Theme: Planting

Texts
Genesis 25:19-34
Psalm 119:105-112
Romans 8:1-11
Matthew 13:1-9, 18-23

Music Of The Day Traditional Hymns
"Open Now Thy Gates Of Beauty" (ELW533, LBW250, GG403)
"Lord Let My Heart Be Good Soil" (ELW512; ccli.com SongSelect)
"My Life Flows On In Endless Song" (ELW763, GG821)
"On Eagle's Wings/You Who Dwell In The Shelter Of The Lord" (ELW787, GG43)
"Blessed Assurance" (ELW638, GG839, UMH369)

Music Of The Day Contemporary Songs
"The Only Name" (Yours Will Be) by Cowart (ccli.com SongSelect)
"Hallelujah" by Brown/Doerksen (ccli.com SongSelect)
"One Thing Remains" by Johnson/Riddle/Black (ccli.com SongSelect)
"Shine" by Ingram/Gonzales (musicnotes.com)
"Know You More" by Zschech (ccli.com SongSelect)

Important Items
The festival of Saint Mary Magdalene is July 22.

Invocation
P   Come and bless us by your presence, + Father, Son, and Holy Spirit and plant good seed into our hearts.
C   Amen.

Confession And Forgiveness
P   Let us approach God, confessing how we are slaves to sin.
(Pause for reflection)
P   Merciful Father,
C   we do not know how to pray as we should. We do not act the ways we want, but do the very evil we don't want. Help us to live according to the Spirit rather than flesh, and take our sin away from us, that we may again bear witness that we are children of God. Amen.

P   Indeed, you are called by the Spirit to be children of God, and by the passion of + Christ you are washed and made new. Together we cry out in thanksgiving.

C   **Abba, Father! Thank you. Amen!**

Apostolic Greeting

P   Inheritors of God's goodness, grace and peace be with you.

C   **And also with you.**

Prayer Of The Day

A   Let us pray. Blessed Lord,

C   **in our wrestling with life and with your presence, offer us a blessing. Make us into the good harvest free from evil and given for the sake of the world and your kingdom. We pray this in the name of your Son, Jesus Christ our Lord. Amen.**

Prayers Of The Church

A   We call out to God in prayer on behalf of those who face all manner of persecution and hardship.

(Pause for reflection)

(After each petition)

A   Come to us, Christ,

C   **and relieve our burdens.**

(If there is a celebratory prayer, use the following instead)

A   Give voice to our joy.

C   **Thanks be to God.**

(After the final petition)

A   By your Spirit, intercede on behalf of those in need with sighs too deep for words.

C   **Amen.**

Offertory Prayer

A   Let us pray. Gracious God,

C   **the gifts you have planted have grown. Now gather these gifts to yourself and grow the kingdom from a small seed into a large tree, and comfort all in the branches of its shelter, through Jesus Christ our Lord. Amen.**

Proper Preface

P   It is indeed our task and celebration to give thanks and praise to you, who pours out the seed, who gives growth in season and who gathers into your kingdom. With those who have been caught and gathered through the ages, we join together in the unending hymn of praise: (Sanctus)

Communion Welcome

P   It is time to be gathered and eat together as a family in Christ.

Post-Communion Blessing

P   May the body and blood of Jesus Christ be a great pearl for your week, a moment of great excitement, and a sign of the kingdom borne out in you.

C   Amen.

Post-Communion Prayer

A   Let us pray. Life-giving Creator,

C   with thanks we take what you have given to us, your very flesh, and we feel your presence still with us. Help us to join together as one in this meal and to bring others to your feast, through our Savior Jesus Christ. Amen.

Benediction

P   You have been given words of life. Go, in the + name of Jesus Christ and carry the living word to the corners of the earth.

C   Amen.

Dismissal

A   Follow the light on your path,

C   with the word as our guide. Amen!

Proper 11 / Ordinary Time 16

Season after Pentecost Theme: Planting

Texts
Genesis 28:10-19a
Psalm 139:1-12, 23-24
Romans 8:12-25
Matthew 13:24-30, 36-43

Music Of The Day Traditional Hymns

"Oh For A Thousand Tongues To Sing" (ELW886, GG610, UMH57, H493)
"Lord Let My Heart Be Good Soil" (ELW512; ccli.com SongSelect)
"Be Thou My Vision" (ELW793, GG450, UMH451, H488)
"Come Let Us Eat" (ELW491, UMH625)
"Praise To The Lord The Almighty" (ELW858, GG35, UMH139, H390)

Music Of The Day Contemporary Songs

"All of Creation" by Millard/Muckala et al (ccli.com SongSelect)
"Holy" by Brown (ccli.com SongSelect)
"The Potter's Hand" by Zschech (ccli.com SongSelect)
"Sing Sing Sing" by Tomlin/Reeves et al (ccli.com SongSelect)
"Communion" by Powell/Avery et al (ccli.com SongSelect)

Important Items

The festival of Saint James the Elder is July 25.

Invocation

P Come and bless us by your presence, + Father, Son, and Holy Spirit and plant good seed into our hearts.
C **Amen.**

Confession And Forgiveness

P Let us approach God, confessing how we are slaves to sin.
(Pause for reflection)
P Merciful Father,
C **we do not know how to pray as we should. We do not act the ways we want, but do the very evil we don't want. Help us to live according to the Spirit rather than flesh, and take our sin away from us, that we may again bear witness that we are children of God. Amen.**

P Indeed, you are called by the Spirit to be children of God, and by the passion of + Christ you are washed and made new. Together we cry out in thanksgiving.

C **Abba, Father! Thank you. Amen!**

Apostolic Greeting

P Inheritors of God's goodness, grace and peace be with you.

C **And also with you.**

Prayer Of The Day

A Let us pray. God of grace,

C **you pour out your word into our hearts and minds. Help us to receive the good news that you offer so that we may in turn tell the old, old story of Jesus and his love. Amen.**

Prayers Of The Church

A We call out to God in prayer on behalf of those who face all manner of persecution and hardship.
(Pause for reflection)
(After each petition)

A Come to us, Christ,

C **and relieve our burdens.**

(If there is a celebratory prayer, use the following instead)

A Give voice to our joy.

C **Thanks be to God.**

(After the final petition)

A By your Spirit, intercede on behalf of those in need with sighs too deep for words.

C **Amen.**

Offertory Prayer

A Let us pray. Gracious God,

C **the gifts you have planted have grown. Now gather these gifts to yourself and grow the kingdom from a small seed into a large tree, and comfort all in the branches of its shelter, through Jesus Christ our Lord. Amen.**

Proper Preface

P It is indeed our task and celebration to give thanks and praise to you, who pours out the seed, who gives growth in season and who gathers into your kingdom. With those who have been caught and gathered through the ages, we join together in the unending hymn of praise: (Sanctus)

Communion Welcome

P It is time to be gathered and eat together as a family in Christ.

Post-Communion Blessing

P   May the body and blood of Jesus Christ be a great pearl for your week, a moment of great excitement, and a sign of the kingdom borne out in you.

C   **Amen.**

Post-Communion Prayer

A   Let us pray. Life-giving Creator,

C   **with thanks we take what you have given to us, your very flesh, and we feel your presence still with us. Help us to join together as one in this meal and to bring others to your feast, through our Savior Jesus Christ. Amen.**

Benediction

P   You have been given words of life. Go, in the + name of Jesus Christ and carry the living Word to the corners of the earth.

C   **Amen.**

Dismissal

A   Follow the light on your path

C   **with the word as our guide. Amen!**

Proper 12 / Ordinary Time 17

Season after Pentecost Theme: Planting

Texts
Genesis 29:15-28
Psalm 105:1-11, 45b
Romans 8:26-39
Matthew 13:31-33, 44-52

Music Of The Day Traditional Hymns
"Here I Am Lord/I The Lord of Sea and Sky" (ELW574, GG69, UMH593)
"Lord Let My Heart Be Good Soil" (ELW512; ccli.com SongSelect)
"Beautiful Savior/Fairest Lord Jesus" (ELW838, GG630, H384)
"One Bread, One Body" (ELW496)
"Go My Children With My Blessing/God That Madest Earth And Heaven" (ELW543, GG547, UMH688)

Music Of The Day Contemporary Songs
"Here To Eternity" by Zschech/Moyse (ccli.com SongSelect)
"God Of Wonders" by Byrd/Hindalong (ccli.com SongSelect)
"How Can I Keep From Singing" by Tomlin/Redman/Cash (ccli.com SongSelect)
"Let Your Kingdom Come" by Fragar (ccli.com SongSelect)
"The Joy Of The Lord" by Paris (ccli.com SongSelect)

Invocation
P Come and bless us by your presence, + Father, Son, and Holy Spirit and plant good seed into our hearts.
C **Amen.**

Confession And Forgiveness
P Let us approach God, confessing how we are slaves to sin.
(Pause for reflection)
P Merciful Father,
C **we do not know how to pray as we should. We do not act the ways we want, but do the very evil we don't want. Help us to live according to the Spirit rather than flesh, and take our sin away from us, that we may again bear witness that we are children of God. Amen.**
P Indeed, you are called by the Spirit to be children of God, and by the passion of + Christ you are washed and made new. Together we cry out in thanksgiving.
C **Abba, Father! Thank you. Amen!**

Apostolic Greeting

P Inheritors of God's goodness, grace and peace be with you.

C **And also with you.**

Prayer Of The Day

A Let us pray. God, our Father,

C **we are blessed that you have called us to be a part of your kingdom. Yet, we know it is not meant just for us. Help us to awaken to the joys of your reign and spread those blessings both far and near, through Jesus Christ our Lord. Amen.**

Prayers Of The Church

A We call out to God in prayer on behalf of those who face all manner of persecution and hardship.
(Pause for reflection)
(After each petition)

A Come to us, Christ,

C **and relieve our burdens.**
(If there is a celebratory prayer, use the following instead)

A Give voice to our joy.

C **Thanks be to God.**
(After the final petition)

A By your Spirit, intercede on behalf of those in need with sighs too deep for words.

C **Amen.**

Offertory Prayer

A Let us pray. Gracious God,

C **the gifts you have planted have grown. Now gather these gifts to yourself and grow the kingdom from a small seed into a large tree, and comfort all in the branches of its shelter, through Jesus Christ our Lord. Amen.**

Proper Preface

P It is indeed our task and celebration to give thanks and praise to you, who pours out the seed, who gives growth in season and who gathers into your kingdom. With those who have been caught and gathered through the ages, we join together in the unending hymn of praise: (Sanctus)

Communion Welcome

P It is time to be gathered and eat together as a family in Christ.

Post-Communion Blessing

P May the body and blood of Jesus Christ be a great pearl for your week, a moment of great excitement, and a sign of the kingdom borne out in you.

C **Amen.**

Post-Communion Prayer

A Let us pray. Life-giving Creator,

C **with thanks we take what you have given to us, your very flesh, and we feel your presence still with us. Help us to join together as one in this meal and to bring others to your feast, through our Savior Jesus Christ. Amen.**

Benediction

P You have been given words of life. Go, in the + name of Jesus Christ and carry the living Word to the corners of the earth.

C **Amen.**

Dismissal

A Follow the light on your path,

C **with the word as our guide. Amen!**

Proper 13 / Ordinary Time 18

Season After Pentecost Theme: Planting

Texts
Genesis 32:22-31
Psalm 17:1-7, 15
Romans 9:1-5
Matthew 14:13-21

Music Of The Day Traditional Hymns
"Holy God We Praise Your Name" (ELW414, GG4, UMH79, H366)
"Lord Let My Heart Be Good Soil" (ELW512; ccli.com SongSelect)
"Eternal Father, Strong To Save" (ELW756, GG8, H608)
"Jesus Loves Me" (ELW595, GG188, UMH191)
"Lead Me, Guide Me" (ELW768, GG740)

Music Of The Day Contemporary Songs
"Whom Shall I Fear? (God of Angel Armies)" by Tomlin/Cash (ccli.com SongSelect)
"Beautiful News" by Redman (ccli.com SongSelect)
"Oceans (Where Feet May Fail)" by Crocker/Houston/Ligthelm (ccli.com SongSelect)
"Hold Me Close" by Paris (ccli.com SongSelect)
"Always" by Stanfill/Ingram (ccli.com SongSelect)

Invocation
P   Praise the Lord, our + God who lives and reigns and works wonders in creation.
C   **Amen.**

Confession And Forgiveness
P   Gathered together as one community let us confess our sins to God.
(Silence for reflection)
P   Gracious God,
C   **we would turn you into who we want you to be. Forgive our arrogance, our selfishness, our anger, our misconceptions, and all other ways that we have failed. Remember your covenant to the generations and show mercy to your children. Amen.**
P   The gifts and calling of God are irrevocable; you who were imprisoned in your sin have been set free to be children of God in the name of the + Father, Son, and Holy Spirit.
C   **Amen.**

Apostolic Greeting

P The grace from God to be free be with you all.

C And also with you.

Prayer Of The Day

A Let us pray. Merciful God,

C we always seek your blessing. Do not send us away until you have fed us and given us all that we need for the sake of your mission in the world, through Jesus Christ our Lord. Amen.

Prayers Of The Church

A As those called by Christ, let us pray for the whole world and its needs.

(Silence for reflection)

(After each petition)

A Messiah of all,

C hear your children's prayer.

(After final petition)

A Hasten to our side, as you have delivered Israel through the ages, Lord, who still reigns over all.

C Amen.

Offertory Prayer

A Let us pray. In thanksgiving, O Lord,

C we raise our voice to you. You have shown your mercy by pouring out gifts over and over again. Now we return these gifts to you so that you may feed the multitudes in ways beyond our comprehension, through Jesus Christ our Savior and Lord. Amen.

Proper Preface

P It is indeed right and our duty to give thanks to you always. With the smallest of gifts you have fed the multitudes, not just with bread and fish but with all that we need for daily life. In remembrance for all you have done, we join with the saints of all times as we sing their unending hymn: (Sanctus)

Communion Welcome

P The bread and wine are prepared. Come, eat, and be filled.

Post-Communion Blessing

P May the body and blood of Jesus Christ cleanse us from the inside out.

C Amen.

Post-Communion Prayer

A Let us pray. Faithful Lord,

C you have once again held true to your word and blessed us by giving your very self. May we be encouraged by your sacrifice to rise up and offer your good news to a world that needs to hear it. Amen.

Benediction

P Blessed + be your feet as you run forward carrying the good news of Jesus Christ our Lord!

C Amen.

Dismissal

A Go and serve in your calling.

C We will, gifted and sent!

Proper 14 / Ordinary Time 19

Season After Pentecost Theme: Planting

Texts
Genesis 37:1-4, 12-28
Psalm 105:1-6, 16-22, 45b
Romans 10:5-15
Matthew 14:22-33

Music Of The Day Traditional Hymns
"Blest Be The Tie That Binds" (ELW656, GG306, UMH557)
"Lord Let My Heart Be Good Soil" (ELW512; ccli.com SongSelect)
"In Christ There Is No East Or West" (ELW650, GG317, UMH548, H529)
"Dear Lord And Father Of Mankind" (ELW506, GG169, UMH358, H652)
"Give To Our God Immortal Praise/From All That Dwell Below The Skies" (ELW848, UMH101)

Music Of The Day Contemporary Songs
"Because Of Your Love" by Baloche/Brown (ccli.com SongSelect)
"Here I Am To Worship" by Hughes (ccli.com SongSelect)
"Forever Reign" by Reeves/Stanfill/Maher at al (ccli.com SongSelect)
"Holy Spirit Rain Down" by Fragar (ccli.com SongSelect)
"Beautiful One" by Hughes (ccli.com SongSelect)

Important Items
The festival of Saint Mary (mother of Jesus) is August 15.

Invocation
P   Praise the Lord, our + God who lives and reigns and works wonders in creation.
C   Amen.

Confession And Forgiveness
P   Gathered together as one community let us confess our sins to God.
(Silence for reflection)
P   Gracious God,
C   we would turn you into who we want you to be. Forgive our arrogance, our selfishness, our anger, our misconceptions, and all other ways that we have failed. Remember your covenant to the generations and show mercy to your children. Amen.

P   The gifts and calling of God are irrevocable; you who were imprisoned in your sin have been set free to be children of God in the name of the + Father, Son, and Holy Spirit.

C   **Amen.**

Apostolic Greeting

P   The grace from God to be free be with you all.

C   **And also with you.**

Prayer Of The Day

A   Let us pray. Awesome God,

C   **reveal yourself to us so that we may have unquestioned faith in you. Give us the words so that we may be assured not just of your love for us, but of your love for all through Jesus Christ our Lord. Amen.**

Prayers Of The Church

A   As those called by Christ, let us pray for the whole world and its needs.

(Silence for reflection)

(After each petition)

A   Messiah of all,

C   **hear your children's prayer.**

(After final petition)

A   Hasten to our side, as you have delivered Israel through the ages, Lord, who still reigns over all.

C   **Amen.**

Offertory Prayer

A   Let us pray. In thanksgiving, O Lord,

C   **we raise our voice to you. You have shown your mercy by pouring out gifts over and over again. Now we return these gifts to you so that you may feed the multitudes in ways beyond our comprehension, through Jesus Christ our Savior and Lord. Amen.**

Proper Preface

P   It is indeed right and our duty to give thanks to you always. With the smallest of gifts you have fed the multitudes, not just with bread and fish but with all that we need for daily life. In remembrance for all you have done, we join with the saints of all times as we sing their unending hymn: (Sanctus)

Communion Welcome

P   The bread and wine are prepared. Come, eat, and be filled.

Post-Communion Blessing

P   May the body and blood of Jesus Christ cleanse us from the inside out.

C   **Amen.**

Post-Communion Prayer

A   Let us pray. Faithful Lord,

C   **you have once again held true to your word and blessed us by giving your very self. May we be encouraged by your sacrifice to rise up and offer your good news to a world that needs to hear it. Amen.**

Benediction

P   Blessed + be your feet as you run forward carrying the good news of Jesus Christ our Lord!

C   **Amen.**

Dismissal

A   Go and serve in your calling.

C   **We will, gifted and sent!**

Proper 15 / Ordinary Time 20

Season After Pentecost Theme: Planting

Texts
Genesis 45:1-15
Psalm 133
Romans 11:1-2a, 29-32
Matthew 15: (10-20) 21-28

Music Of The Day Traditional Hymns
"O For A Thousand Tongues To Sing" (ELW886, GG610, UMH57, H493)
"Lord Let My Heart Be Good Soil" (ELW512; ccli.com SongSelect)
"The Church's One Foundation" (ELW654, GG321, UMH545, H525)
"Healer Of Our Every Ill" (ELW612)
"I Love To Tell The Story" (ELW661, GG462, UMH156)

Music Of The Day Contemporary Songs
"All Things Are Possible" by Zschech (ccli.com SongSelect)
"Indescribable" by Story (ccli.com SongSelect)
"Jesus Messiah" by Carson/Tomlin et al (ccli.com SongSelect)
"Faith" by Morgan (ccli.com SongSelect)
"Unfailing Love" by Tomlin/Pierce/Cash (ccli.com SongSelect)

Important Items
The festival of Saint Bartholomew is August 24.

Invocation
P Praise the Lord, our + God who lives and reigns and works wonders in creation.
C **Amen.**

Confession And Forgiveness
P Gathered together as one community let us confess our sins to God.
(Silence for reflection)
P Gracious God,
C **we would turn you into who we want you to be. Forgive our arrogance, our selfishness, our anger, our misconceptions, and all other ways that we have failed. Remember your covenant to the generations and show mercy to your children. Amen.**

P The gifts and calling of God are irrevocable; you who were imprisoned in your sin have been set free to be children of God in the name of the + Father, Son, and Holy Spirit.

C **Amen.**

Apostolic Greeting

P The grace from God to be free be with you all.

C **And also with you.**

Prayer Of The Day

A Let us pray. Gracious Savior,

C **keep our eyes open and on the watch to find the moments of grace that you send into the world, even through those people and places we don't normally consider to be blessed. Amen.**

Prayers Of The Church

A As those called by Christ, let us pray for the whole world and its needs.

(Silence for reflection)

(After each petition)

A Messiah of all,

C **hear your children's prayer.**

(After final petition)

A Hasten to our side, as you have delivered Israel through the ages, Lord, who still reigns over all.

C **Amen.**

Offertory Prayer

A Let us pray. In thanksgiving, O Lord,

C **we raise our voice to you. You have shown your mercy by pouring out gifts over and over again. Now we return these gifts to you so that you may feed the multitudes in ways beyond our comprehension, through Jesus Christ our Savior and Lord. Amen.**

Proper Preface

P It is indeed right and our duty to give thanks to you always. With the smallest of gifts you have fed the multitudes, not just with bread and fish but with all that we need for daily life. In remembrance for all you have done, we join with the saints of all times as we sing their unending hymn: (Sanctus)

Communion Welcome

P The bread and wine are prepared. Come, eat, and be filled.

Post-Communion Blessing

P May the body and blood of Jesus Christ cleanse us from the inside out.

C **Amen.**

Post-Communion Prayer

A Let us pray. Faithful Lord,

C **you have once again held true to your word and blessed us by giving your very self. May we be encouraged by your sacrifice to rise up and offer your good news to a world that needs to hear it. Amen.**

Benediction

P Blessed + be your feet as you run forward carrying the good news of Jesus Christ our Lord!

C **Amen.**

Dismissal

A Go and serve in your calling.

C **We will, gifted and sent!**

Proper 16 / Ordinary Time 21

Season After Pentecost Theme: Planting

Texts
Exodus 1:8-2:10
Psalm 124
Romans 12:1-8
Matthew 16:13-20

Music Of The Day Traditional Hymns
"O Savior, Precious Savior/O Jesus I Have Promised" (ELW820, LBW514, GG724, UMH396)
"Shout To The Lord" (ELW821; ccli.com SongSelect)
"Lord Let My Heart Be Good Soil" (ELW512; ccli.com SongSelect)
"For The Bread Which You Have Broken" (ELW494, GG516, H341)
"Seek Ye First" (WOV783, GG175, UMH405, H711)
"What A Friend We Have In Jesus" (ELW742, GG465, UMH526)

Music Of The Day Contemporary Songs
"Hear Our Praises" by Morgan (ccli.com SongSelect)
"Come, Let Us Worship" by Reeves/Tomlin (ccli.com SongSelect)
"How Can I Keep From Singing?" by Tomlin/Redman/Cash et al (ccli.com SongSelect)
"God Of This City" by Boyd/Bleakly et al (ccli.com SongSelect)
"Take My Life" by Tomlin/Giglio (ccli.com SongSelect)

Invocation
P   Praise the Lord, our + God who lives and reigns and works wonders in creation.
C   Amen.

Confession And Forgiveness
P   Gathered together as one community let us confess our sins to God.
(Silence for reflection)
P   Gracious God,
C   we would turn you into who we want you to be. Forgive our arrogance, our selfishness, our anger, our misconceptions, and all other ways that we have failed. Remember your covenant to the generations and show mercy to your children. Amen.
P   The gifts and calling of God are irrevocable; you who were imprisoned in your sin have been set free to be children of God in the name of the + Father, Son, and Holy Spirit.
C   Amen.

Apostolic Greeting

P The grace from God to be free be with you all.

C And also with you.

Prayer Of The Day

A Let us pray. Holy Father,

C you send salvation for our needs even in small packages. Give us wisdom and insight to call you Lord and to trust that you are always and will always be drawing us into new life, through Jesus Christ our Lord. Amen.

Prayers Of The Church

A As those called by Christ, let us pray for the whole world and its needs.

(Silence for reflection)

(After each petition)

A Messiah of all,

C hear your children's prayer.

(After final petition)

A Hasten to our side, as you have delivered Israel through the ages, Lord, who still reigns over all.

C Amen.

Offertory Prayer

A Let us pray. In thanksgiving, O Lord,

C we raise our voice to you. You have shown your mercy by pouring out gifts over and over again. Now we return these gifts to you so that you may feed the multitudes in ways beyond our comprehension, through Jesus Christ our Savior and Lord. Amen.

Proper Preface

P It is indeed right and our duty to give thanks to you always. With the smallest of gifts you have fed the multitudes, not just with bread and fish but with all that we need for daily life. In remembrance for all you have done, we join with the saints of all times as we sing their unending hymn: (Sanctus)

Communion Welcome

P The bread and wine are prepared. Come, eat, and be filled.

Post-Communion Blessing

P May the body and blood of Jesus Christ cleanse us from the inside out.

C Amen.

Post-Communion Prayer

A   Let us pray. Faithful Lord,

C   you have once again held true to your word and blessed us by giving your very self. May we be encouraged by your sacrifice to rise up and offer your good news to a world that needs to hear it. Amen.

Benediction

P   Blessed + be your feet as you run forward carrying the good news of Jesus Christ our Lord!

C   Amen.

Dismissal

A   Go and serve in your calling.

C   We will, gifted and sent!

Season After Pentecost Theme: Harvesting

Texts
Exodus 3:1-15
Psalm 105:1-6, 23-26, 45b
Romans 12:9-21
Matthew 16:21-28

Music Of The Day Traditional Hymns
"Lift High The Cross/Come Christians Follow" (ELW660, GG826, UMH159)
"Love Divine, All Loves Excelling" (ELW631, GG366, UMH384b, H657)
"How Great Thou Art" (ELW856, GG625, UMH77)
"As The Grains Of Wheat" (ELW465)
"Earth And All Stars" (ELW731, GG26)
"O Sing To The Lord" (ELW822, WOV795, GG637)

Music Of The Day Contemporary Songs
"Come To The Cross" by Smith (ccli.com SongSelect)
"Beautiful One" by Hughes (ccli.com SongSelect)
"Eternal Word" by Linda Holcombe
"You Alone" by Parker/Crowder (ccli.com SongSelect)
"Greater" by Graul/Millard et al (praisecharts.com)
"Communion" by Powell/Avery et al (ccli.com SongSelect)

Important Items
Labor Day

Invocation
P Come to us, great + I Am, and greet us as we worship you.
C Amen.

Confession And Forgiveness
P Let us stand together before the judgment seat of God and confess our sins
(Silence for reflection)
P Righteous Christ,

C we have errantly judged one another, and we have worried more about the sins of others than our own. Help us repent of these and all other sins we commit so that we may focus our hearts and minds on the goals of your kingdom. Amen.

P The Lord reaches out in compassion, forgiving beyond our capacity to reason. You have been forgiven in the name of the + Father, Son, and Holy Spirit.

C Amen.

Apostolic Greeting

P May the bountiful gifts of God tend to your needs.

C Amen.

Prayer Of The Day

A Let us pray. Son of man,

C guide us into the way of peace. Help us to know what it means to worship you both in our own lives and in our time spent in service to our neighbor. Grant this in your holy name. Amen.

Prayers Of The Church

A As a unified community let us pray for all in need, even those who persecute us.

(Silence for reflection)

(After each petition)

A For these and all needs,

C give us our daily bread.

(After final petition)

A As you fed those in the wilderness with the bread from heaven, continue to feed all who hunger and are in need, through Jesus Christ our Lord.

C Amen.

Offertory Prayer

A Let us pray. Gracious Father,

C when your people are in need, you provide. As you have given us gifts for our journeys, we now return those gifts to you. Make us into hope for a weary world, and use these blessings for the sake of those in need. We ask this mission and blessing through Jesus, your only Son, our Lord. Amen.

Proper Preface

P In remembering your blessings we give thanks and praise for all the work you have done on our behalf. You led our ancestors by fire and smoke, you fed them and gave them water. As we acknowledge the ways you care for us we join together with those who have relied on you throughout the ages as we join in the unending hymn. (Sanctus)

Communion Welcome

P   Bread from heaven is laid out before you. Come, eat, and live.

Post-Communion Blessing

P   May this bread and wine be all that we need to be faithful laborers in the vineyard.

C **Amen.**

Post-Communion Prayer

A   Let us pray. Loving Christ,

C **our souls are filled with your love for us. May this meal serve as a way to remember your faithfulness and may it draw us out to love the whole world with the passion you show to us in Jesus Christ our Savior. Amen.**

Benediction

P   May you live peaceably with all, sheltered and encouraged by the gifts of the + Father, Son, and Holy Spirit.

C **Amen.**

Dismissal

A   Go forth and overcome evil with good.

C **Thanks be to God. Amen!**

Proper 18 / Ordinary Time 23

Season After Pentecost Theme: Harvesting

Texts
Exodus 12:1-14
Psalm 149
Romans 13:8-14
Matthew 18:15-20

Music Of The Day Traditional Hymns

"I Come With Joy" (ELW482, GG515, UMH617)
"O God Beyond All Praising/O God Show Mercy To Us" (ELW880, GG341)
"Praise My Soul The God Of Heaven/Praise My Soul The King Of Heaven" (ELW864, GG620, UMH66, H410)
"As The Grains Of Wheat" (ELW465)
"Let Us Break Bread Together" (ELW471, GG525, UMH618, H325)
"Joyful, Joyful, We Adore Thee" (ELW836, LBW551, GG611, UMH89, H376)

Music Of The Day Contemporary Songs

"Everlasting God" by Brown/Riley (ccli.com SongSelect)
"God Of Wonders" by Byrd/Hindalong (ccli.com SongSelect)
"Eternal Word" by Linda Holcombe
"Made To Worship" by Tomlin/Sharp/Cash (ccli.com SongSelect)
"Amazing Grace (My Chains Are Gone)" by Newton/Tomlin et al (ccli.com SongSelect)
"One Hope" by Zschech (ccli.com SongSelect)

Important Items

Grandparents' Day

The remembrance of September 11 attacks is this week.

The Feast of the Holy Cross is September 14.

Invocation

P Come to us, great + I Am, and greet us as we worship you.
C Amen.

Confession And Forgiveness

P   Let us stand together before the judgment seat of God and confess our sins.

(Silence for reflection)

P   Righteous Christ,

C   **we have errantly judged one another, and we have worried more about the sins of others than our own. Help us repent of these and all other sins we commit so that we may focus our hearts and minds on the goals of your kingdom. Amen.**

P   The Lord reaches out in compassion, forgiving beyond our capacity to reason. You have been forgiven in the name of the + Father, Son, and Holy Spirit.

C   **Amen.**

Apostolic Greeting

P   May the bountiful gifts of God tend to your needs.

C   **Amen.**

Prayer Of The Day

A   Let us pray. Ever-present Christ,

C   **draw us into your Spirit that we may with all that we say, do, and think offer and return praise to you. Help focus our mind on divine things to build up the community, in your name we pray. Amen.**

Prayers Of The Church

A   As a unified community let us pray for all in need, even those who persecute us.

(Silence for reflection)

(After each petition)

A   For these and all needs,

C   **give us our daily bread.**

(After final petition)

A   As you fed those in the wilderness with the bread from heaven, continue to feed all who hunger and are in need, through Jesus Christ our Lord.

C   **Amen.**

Offertory Prayer

A   Let us pray. Gracious Father,

C   **when your people are in need, you provide. As you have given us gifts for our journeys, we now return those gifts to you. Make us into hope for a weary world, and use these blessings for the sake of those in need. We ask this mission and blessing through Jesus, your only Son, our Lord. Amen.**

Proper Preface

P   In remembering your blessings we give thanks and praise for all the work you have done on our behalf. You led our ancestors by fire and smoke, you fed them and gave them water. As we acknowledge the ways you care for us we join together with those who have relied on you throughout the ages as we join in the unending hymn. (Sanctus)

Communion Welcome

P   Bread from heaven is laid out before you. Come, eat, and live.

Post-Communion Blessing

P   May this bread and wine be all that we need to be faithful laborers in the vineyard.
C   **Amen.**

Post-Communion Prayer

A   Let us pray. Loving Christ,
C   **our souls are filled with your love for us. May this meal serve as a way to remember your faithfulness and may it draw us out to love the whole world with the passion you show to us in Jesus Christ our Savior. Amen.**

Benediction

P   May you live peaceably with all, sheltered and encouraged by the gifts of the + Father, Son, and Holy Spirit.
C   **Amen.**

Dismissal

A   Go forth and overcome evil with good.
C   **Thanks be to God. Amen!**

Season After Pentecost Theme: Harvesting

Texts
Exodus 14:19-31
Psalm 114
Romans 14:1-12
Matthew 18:21-35

Music Of The Day Traditional Hymns
"Glories Of Your Name Are Spoken/Glorious Things Of Thee Are Spoken" (LBW358, GG81, UMH731, H522)
"Take My Life That I May Be" (ELW685, GG697, UMH399, H707)
"When We Are Living" (ELW639, GG822, UMH356)
"As The Grains Of Wheat" (ELW465)
"Softly And Tenderly Jesus Is Calling" (ELW608, GG418, UMH348)
"For The Fruit Of All Creation" (ELW679, GG36, UMH97b, H424)

Music Of The Day Contemporary Songs
"This Is Amazing Grace" by Wickham (ccli.com SongSelect)
"Blessed Be Your Name" by Redman (ccli.com SongSelect)
"Eternal Word" by Linda Holcombe
"That's Why We Praise Him" by Walker (ccli.com SongSelect)
"Build Your Kingdom Here" by Rend Collective Experiment (ccli.com SongSelect)
"Know You More" by Zschech (ccli.com SongSelect)

Important Items
The festival for Saint Matthew is September 21.

Native American Day is September 22.

Invocation
P   Come to us, great + I Am, and greet us as we worship you.
C   **Amen.**

Confession And Forgiveness
P   Let us stand together before the judgment seat of God and confess our sins.

(Silence for reflection)

P   Righteous Christ,

C   **we have errantly judged one another, and we have worried more about the sins of others than our own. Help us repent of these and all other sins we commit so that we may focus our hearts and minds on the goals of your kingdom. Amen.**

P   The Lord reaches out in compassion, forgiving beyond our capacity to reason. You have been forgiven in the name of the + Father, Son, and Holy Spirit.

C   **Amen.**

Apostolic Greeting

P   May the bountiful gifts of God tend to your needs.

C   **Amen.**

Prayer Of The Day

A   Let us pray. Merciful God,

C   **teach us to understand forgiveness. Help us to know that we are forgiven and how that changes our hearts and how we engage the world. Continue to forgive us as we learn how to forgive others in the name of Jesus Christ our Savior. Amen.**

Prayers Of The Church

A   As a unified community let us pray for all in need, even those who persecute us.

(Silence for reflection)

(After each petition)

A   For these and all needs,

C   **give us our daily bread.**

(After final petition)

A   As you fed those in the wilderness with the bread from heaven, continue to feed all who hunger and are in need, through Jesus Christ our Lord.

C   **Amen.**

Offertory Prayer

A   Let us pray. Gracious Father,

C   **when your people are in need, you provide. As you have given us gifts for our journeys, we now return those gifts to you. Make us into hope for a weary world, and use these blessings for the sake of those in need. We ask this mission and blessing through Jesus, your only Son, our Lord. Amen.**

Proper Preface

P   In remembering your blessings we give thanks and praise for all the work you have done on our behalf. You led our ancestors by fire and smoke, you fed them and gave them water. As we acknowledge the ways you care for us we join together with those who have relied on you throughout the ages as we join in the unending hymn. (Sanctus)

Communion Welcome

P   Bread from heaven is laid out before you. Come, eat, and live.

Post-Communion Blessing

P   May this bread and wine be all that we need to be faithful laborers in the vineyard.

C   **Amen.**

Post-Communion Prayer

A   Let us pray. Loving Christ,

C   **our souls are filled with your love for us. May this meal serve as a way to remember your faithfulness and may it draw us out to love the whole world with the passion you show to us in Jesus Christ our Savior. Amen.**

Benediction

P   May you live peaceably with all, sheltered and encouraged by the gifts of the + Father, Son, and Holy Spirit.

C   **Amen.**

Dismissal

A   Go forth and overcome evil with good.

C   **Thanks be to God. Amen!**

Proper 20 / Ordinary Time 25

Season After Pentecost Theme: Harvesting

Texts
Exodus 16:2-15
Psalm 105:1-6, 37-45
Philippians 1:21-30
Matthew 20:1-16

Music Of The Day Traditional Hymns
"Stand Up, Stand Up For Jesus" (LBW389, UMH514, H561)
"I Love Your Kingdom, Lord" (LBW368, GG310, UMH540, H524)
"Blessed Assurance" (ELW638, GG839, UMH369)
"As The Grains Of Wheat" (ELW465)
"I Received The Living God" (ELW477)
"O For A Thousand Tongues To Sing" (ELW886, GG610, UMH57, H493)

Music Of The Day Contemporary Songs
"Here To Eternity by Zschech/Moyse" (ccli.com SongSelect)
"Come Now Is The Time To Worship" by Doerksen (ccli.com SongSelect)
"Eternal Word" by Linda Holcombe
"Open The Eyes Of My Heart" by Baloche (ccli.com SongSelect)
"He Reigns" by Furler/Taylor (ccli.com SongSelect)
"Let Your Kingdom Come" by Fragar (ccli.com SongSelect)

Important Items
The festival for Saint Michael and All Angels is September 29.

Invocation
P Come to us, great + I Am, and greet us as we worship you.
C **Amen.**

Confession And Forgiveness
P Let us stand together before the judgment seat of God and confess our sins.
(Silence for reflection)
P Righteous Christ,

C we have errantly judged one another, and we have worried more about the sins of others than our own. Help us repent of these and all other sins we commit so that we may focus our hearts and minds on the goals of your kingdom. Amen.

P The Lord reaches out in compassion, forgiving beyond our capacity to reason. You have been forgiven in the name of the + Father, Son, and Holy Spirit.

C Amen.

Apostolic Greeting

P May the bountiful gifts of God tend to your needs.

C Amen.

Prayer Of The Day

A Let us pray. God of the harvest,

C make us into your laborers. Lead us with your good news that we may go into the world and draw out goodness and love even in the face of suffering. We pray this in Jesus Christ's name. Amen.

Prayers Of The Church

A As a unified community let us pray for all in need, even those who persecute us.

(Silence for reflection)

(After each petition)

A For these and all needs,

C give us our daily bread.

(After final petition)

A As you fed those in the wilderness with the bread from heaven, continue to feed all who hunger and are in need, through Jesus Christ our Lord.

C Amen.

Offertory Prayer

A Let us pray. Gracious Father,

C when your people are in need, you provide. As you have given us gifts for our journeys, we now return those gifts to you. Make us into hope for a weary world, and use these blessings for the sake of those in need. We ask this mission and blessing through Jesus, your only Son, our Lord. Amen.

Proper Preface

P In remembering your blessings we give thanks and praise for all the work you have done on our behalf. You led our ancestors by fire and smoke, you fed them and gave them water. As we acknowledge the ways you care for us we join together with those who have relied on you throughout the ages as we join in the unending hymn. (Sanctus)

Communion Welcome

P Bread from heaven is laid out before you. Come, eat, and live.

Post-Communion Blessing

P May this bread and wine be all that we need to be faithful laborers in the vineyard.

C **Amen.**

Post-Communion Prayer

A Let us pray. Loving Christ,

C **our souls are filled with your love for us. May this meal serve as a way to remember your faithfulness and may it draw us out to love the whole world with the passion you show to us in Jesus Christ our Savior. Amen.**

Benediction

P May you live peaceably with all, sheltered and encouraged by the gifts of the + Father, Son, and Holy Spirit.

C **Amen.**

Dismissal

A Go forth and overcome evil with good.

C **Thanks be to God. Amen!**

Proper 21 / Ordinary Time 26

Season After Pentecost Theme: Harvesting

Texts
Exodus 17:1-7
Psalm 78:1-4, 12-16
Philippians 2:1-13
Matthew 21:23-32

Music Of The Day Traditional Hymns

"Here In This Place (Gather Us In)" (ELW532, WOV718, GG401)
"Come Thou Fount Of Every Blessing" (ELW807, GG475, UMH400, H686)
"This Is My Father's World" (ELW824, GG370, UMH144, H651)
"As The Grains Of Wheat" (ELW465)
"For The Beauty Of The Earth" (ELW879, GG14, UMH92, H416)
"What A Fellowship, What A Joy Divine" (ELW774, GG837, UMH133)

Music Of The Day Contemporary Songs

"Shout For Joy" by Baloche/Brewster/Ingram (ccli.com SongSelect)
"Forever" by Tomlin (ccli.com SongSelect)
"Eternal Word" by Linda Holcombe
"Cornerstone" by Myrin/Morgan (ccli.com SongSelect)
"We Believe" by Ryan/Fike/Hooper (ccli.com SongSelect)
"You Are Holy" by Paris (ccli.com SongSelect)

Invocation

P   Dwell with us this day, Son of heaven, and send your Spirit to be in our hearts.
C   **Amen.**

Confession And Forgiveness

P   Gather at the foot of God's mountain and we'll confess together our sins in God's presence.
(Silence for reflection)
P   Great law-giver,
C   **we have failed to even uphold the easiest of commandments and our lives are in desperate need of your intervention. Speak directly to our hearts and cleanse them from the sin that clings closely. Pass your mercy to us for the sake of your Son who died for us, Jesus Christ. Amen.**

P   Through your faith in Christ, his righteousness cloaks you. Beloved saints, your sins are forgiven in the name of the + Father, Son, and Holy Spirit.

C   **Amen.**

Apostolic Greeting

P   Grace and peace be with you, beloved in Christ.

C   **And also with you.**

Prayer Of The Day

A   Let us pray. Righteous God,

C   **we say one thing and do another. Make our words and actions line up. Call us each to newness of life given away for the sake of others and not for our own self-interest, through Jesus our way, truth, and life. Amen.**

Prayers Of The Church

A   Let us stand up on behalf of the people of God to ask for God's blessings

(Silence for reflection)

(After each petition)

A   For those who need your care

C   **we lift up our voice.**

(After final petition)

A   Remember your covenant to our ancestors and grant blessings in abundance for all who find themselves in need this day, through Jesus Christ our Lord.

C   **Amen.**

Offertory Prayer

A   Let us pray. Holy God,

C   **your power has been shown across the earth, and the signs are in these gifts we return to you. Help us to let you continue to work through our hands and bless their work so that all we bring back to you may bring new life to those in need. Amen.**

Proper Preface

P   It is our duty and joy that we offer to you our thanks and praise for the myriad of works you have shown to your people. Your hand guided even when we were rebellious and still continues this day to guide us back to the communion of all saints, with whom we join in the unending hymn: (Sanctus)

Communion Welcome

P   The bread and wine from heaven are given as a gift for you.

Post-Communion Blessing

P As the body and blood of Christ move in your own body, may they strengthen and unite us all in unity of mission.

C **Amen.**

Post-Communion Prayer

A Let us pray. Life-giving Lord,

C **you have fed your family with the true gifts of your sacrifice. Let your passion enflame our hearts that we may reach out in love and service to all whom we meet; in your holy name we pray. Amen.**

Benediction

P May Christ place in your hearts and minds that which was in Christ Jesus: sacrifice, mercy, and love.

C **Amen.**

Dismissal

A Go and tend to the vineyard of the world.

C **We will, ready to greet all in the name of Christ!**

Proper 22 / Ordinary Time 27

Season After Pentecost Theme: Harvesting

Texts
Exodus 20:1-4, 7-9, 12-20
Psalm 19
Philippians 3:4b-14
Matthew 21:33-46

Music Of The Day Traditional Hymns
"Rise Up, O Saints Of God" (LBW383, UMH576, H551)
"Here I Am Lord/I The Lord Of Sea And Sky" (ELW574, GG69, UMH593)
"My Song Is Love Unknown" (ELW343, WOV661, GG209, H458)
"As The Grains Of Wheat" (ELW465)
"I Am The Bread Of Life" (ELW485, GG522, H335)
"O God Our Help In Ages Past" (ELW632, GG687, UMH117, H680)

Music Of The Day Contemporary Songs
"All Over The World" by Redman/Smith (ccli.com SongSelect)
"Hallelujah" by Brown/Doerksen (ccli.com SongSelect)
"Eternal Word" by Linda Holcombe
"How Great Is Our God" by Tomlin/Reeves/Cash (ccli.com SongSelect)
"What A Savior" by Jones/Story (ccli.com SongSelect)
"Remembrance (The Communion Song)" by Maher/Redman (ccli.com SongSelect)

Important Items
Now would be a good week to begin to gather names for All Saints' Sunday.

Columbus Day

Invocation
P   Dwell with us this day, Son of heaven, and send your Spirit to be in our hearts.
C   **Amen.**

Confession And Forgiveness
P   Gather at the foot of God's mountain, and we'll confess together our sins in God's presence.

(Silence for reflection)

P   Great law-giver,

C   **we have failed to even uphold the easiest of commandments and our lives are in desperate need of your intervention. Speak directly to our hearts and cleanse them from the sin that clings closely. Pass your mercy to us for the sake of your Son who died for us, Jesus Christ. Amen.**

P   Through your faith in Christ, his righteousness cloaks you. Beloved saints, your sins are forgiven in the name of the + Father, Son, and Holy Spirit.

C   **Amen.**

Apostolic Greeting

P   Grace and peace be with you, beloved in Christ.

C   **And also with you.**

Prayer Of The Day

A   Let us pray. Eternal Lord,

C   **though your faithfulness is static, the way you reveal yourself has often caught us unaware. Help us to lift up those places and people who bear your name and carry your commandments. Amen.**

Prayers Of The Church

A   Let us stand up on behalf of the people of God to ask for God's blessings.

(Silence for reflection)

(After each petition)

A   For those who need your care,

C   **we lift up our voice.**

(After final petition)

A   Remember your covenant to our ancestors and grant blessings in abundance for all who find themselves in need this day, through Jesus Christ our Lord.

C   **Amen.**

Offertory Prayer

A   Let us pray. Holy God,

C   **your power has been shown across the earth, and the signs are in these gifts we return to you. Help us to let you continue to work through our hands and bless their work so that all we bring back to you may bring new life to those in need. Amen.**

Proper Preface

P   It is our duty and joy that we offer to you our thanks and praise for the myriad of works you have shown to your people. Your hand guided even when we were rebellious and still continues this day to guide us back to the communion of all saints, with whom we join in the unending hymn. (Sanctus)

Communion Welcome

P The bread and wine from heaven are given as a gift for you.

Post-Communion Blessing

P As the body and blood of Christ move in your own body, may they strengthen and unite us all in unity of mission.

C **Amen.**

Post-Communion Prayer

A Let us pray. Life-giving Lord,

C **you have fed your family with the true gifts of your sacrifice. Let your passion enflame our hearts that we may reach out in love and service to all whom we meet; in your holy name we pray. Amen.**

Benediction

P May Christ place in your hearts and minds that which was in Christ Jesus: sacrifice, mercy, and love.

C **Amen.**

Dismissal

A Go and tend to the vineyard of the world.

C **We will, ready to greet all in the name of Christ!**

Proper 23 / Ordinary Time 28

Season After Pentecost Theme: Harvesting

Texts
Exodus 32:1-14
Psalm 106:1-6, 19-23
Philippians 4:1-9
Matthew 22:1-14

Music Of The Day Traditional Hymns
"Come, You/Ye Thankful People, Come" (ELW693, LBW407, GG367, UMH694, H290)
"If You But Trust In God To Guide You/If Thou But Suffer God To Guide Thee" (ELW769, LBW453, GG816, UMH142, H635)
"My Life Flows On In Endless Song" (ELW763, GG821)
"As The Grains Of Wheat" (ELW465)
"Break Now/Thou The Bread Of Life" (ELW515, LBW235, GG460, UMH599)
"Amazing Grace" (ELW779, GG649, UMH378, H671)

Music Of The Day Contemporary Songs
"The Only Name (Yours Will Be)" by Cowart (ccli.com SongSelect)
"Dwell In Your House" by Ewing (ccli.com SongSelect)
"Eternal Word" by Linda Holcombe
"Amazing Grace" (ccli.com SongSelect)
"You Are" by Roach (ccli.com SongSelect)
"You Are Holy" by Paris (ccli.com SongSelect)

Important Items
The festival for Saint Luke is October 18.

Invocation
P   Dwell with us this day, Son of heaven, and send your Spirit to be in our hearts.
C   **Amen.**

Confession And Forgiveness
P   Gather at the foot of God's mountain, and we'll confess together our sins in God's presence.
(Silence for reflection)

P Great law-giver,

C **we have failed to even uphold the easiest of commandments and our lives are in desperate need of your intervention. Speak directly to our hearts and cleanse them from the sin that clings closely. Pass your mercy to us for the sake of your Son who died for us, Jesus Christ. Amen.**

P Through your faith in Christ, his righteousness cloaks you. Beloved saints, your sins are forgiven in the name of the + Father, Son, and Holy Spirit.

C **Amen.**

Apostolic Greeting

P Grace and peace be with you, beloved in Christ.

C **And also with you.**

Prayer Of The Day

A Let us pray. God most high,

C **in fear we turn away and seek other gods. Help us to always call you Lord and be ready for when you call us to your service, through our Lord and Savior Jesus Christ. Amen.**

Prayers Of The Church

A Let us stand up on behalf of the people of God to ask for God's blessings.

(Silence for reflection)

(After each petition)

A For those who need your care,

C **we lift up our voice.**

(After final petition)

A Remember your covenant to our ancestors and grant blessings in abundance for all who find themselves in need this day, through Jesus Christ our Lord.

C **Amen.**

Offertory Prayer

A Let us pray. Holy God,

C **your power has been shown across the earth, and the signs are in these gifts we return to you. Help us to let you continue to work through our hands and bless their work so that all we bring back to you may bring new life to those in need. Amen.**

Proper Preface

P It is our duty and joy that we offer to you our thanks and praise for the myriad of works you have shown to your people. Your hand guided even when we were rebellious and still continues this day to guide us back to the communion of all saints, with whom we join in the unending hymn: (Sanctus)

Communion Welcome

P The bread and wine from heaven are given as a gift for you.

Post-Communion Blessing

P   As the body and blood of Christ move in your own body, may they strengthen and unite us all in unity of mission.

C   **Amen.**

Post-Communion Prayer

A   Let us pray. Life-giving Lord,

C   **you have fed your family with the true gifts of your sacrifice. Let your passion enflame our hearts that we may reach out in love and service to all whom we meet; in your holy name we pray. Amen.**

Benediction

P   May Christ place in your hearts and minds that which was in Christ Jesus: sacrifice, mercy, and love.

C   **Amen.**

Dismissal

A   Go and tend to the vineyard of the world.

C   **We will, ready to greet all in the name of Christ!**

Proper 24 / Ordinary Time 29

Season After Pentecost Theme: Harvesting

Texts
Exodus 33:12-23
Psalm 99
1 Thessalonians 1:1-10
Matthew 22:15-22

Music Of The Day Traditional Hymns
"God of Grace And God of Glory" (ELW705, GG307, UMH577, H594)
"We Give Thee But Thine Own" (ELW686, LBW410, GG708)
"What A Friend We Have In Jesus" (ELW742, GG465, UMH526)
"As The Grains Of Wheat" (ELW465)
"Songs Of Thankfulness And Praise" (ELW310, H135)
"Jesus Shall Reign" (ELW434, GG265, UMH157, H544, LBW530)

Music Of The Day Contemporary Songs
"Faith" by Morgan (ccli.com SongSelect)
"The Joy Of The Lord" by Paris (ccli.com SongSelect)
"Eternal Word" by Linda Holcombe
"This Is The Day" by Fitts (ccli.com SongSelect)
"To God Alone" by Shust/Ingram (ccli.com SongSelect)
"You Are Holy" by Paris (ccli.com SongSelect)

Important Items
The festival for Saint Simon and Saint Jude is October 28.

Remind people to wear red for Reformation Day next week.

Invocation
P   Dwell with us this day, Son of heaven, and send your Spirit to be in our hearts.
C   Amen.

Confession And Forgiveness
P   Gather at the foot of God's mountain, and we'll confess together our sins in God's presence.

(Silence for reflection)

P   Great law-giver,

C   **we have failed to even uphold the easiest of commandments and our lives are in desperate need of your intervention. Speak directly to our hearts and cleanse them from the sin that clings closely. Pass your mercy to us for the sake of your Son who died for us, Jesus Christ. Amen.**

P   Through your faith in Christ, his righteousness cloaks you. Beloved saints, your sins are forgiven in the name of the + Father, Son, and Holy Spirit.

C   **Amen.**

Apostolic Greeting

P   Grace and peace be with you, beloved in Christ.

C   **And also with you.**

Prayer Of The Day

A   Let us pray. Merciful God,

C   **your blessings are all around. Help us to return what is yours: our whole selves. May we give all over to you so that your word may surround us and your light shine through us. Amen.**

Prayers Of The Church

A   Let us stand up on behalf of the people of God to ask for God's blessings.

(Silence for reflection)

(After each petition)

A   For those who need your care,

C   **we lift up our voice.**

(After final petition)

A   Remember your covenant to our ancestors and grant blessings in abundance for all who find themselves in need this day, through Jesus Christ our Lord.

C   **Amen.**

Offertory Prayer

A   Let us pray. Holy God,

C   **your power has been shown across the earth, and the signs are in these gifts we return to you. Help us to let you continue to work through our hands and bless their work so that all we bring back to you may bring new life to those in need. Amen.**

Proper Preface

P   It is our duty and joy that we offer to you our thanks and praise for the myriad of works you have shown to your people. Your hand guided even when we were rebellious and still continues this day to guide us back to the communion of all saints, with whom we join in the unending hymn. (Sanctus)

Communion Welcome

P   The bread and wine from heaven are given as a gift for you.

Post-Communion Blessing

P   As the body and blood of Christ move in your own body, may they strengthen and unite us all in unity of mission.

C   **Amen.**

Post-Communion Prayer

A   Let us pray. Life-giving Lord,

C   **you have fed your family with the true gifts of your sacrifice. Let your passion enflame our hearts that we may reach out in love and service to all whom we meet; in your holy name we pray. Amen.**

Benediction

P   May Christ place in your hearts and minds that which was in Christ Jesus: sacrifice, mercy, and love.

C   **Amen.**

Dismissal

A   Go and tend to the vineyard of the world.

C   **We will, ready to greet all in the name of Christ!**

Proper 25 / Ordinary Time 30

Season After Pentecost Theme: Harvesting

Texts
Deuteronomy 34:1-12
Psalm 90:1-6, 13-17
1 Thessalonians 2:1-8
Matthew 22:34-46

Music Of The Day Traditional Hymns
"We Are Called" (ELW720)
"Be Thou My Vision" (ELW793, GG450, UMH451, H488)
"Children Of The Heavenly Father" (ELW781, UMH141)
"As The Grains Of Wheat" (ELW465)
"Seek Ye First" (WOV783, GG175, UMH405, H711)
"Love Divine, All Loves Excelling" (ELW631, GG366, UMH384b, H657)

Music Of The Day Contemporary Songs
"Hear Our Praises" by Morgan (ccli.com SongSelect)
"Love The Lord" by Brewster (ccli.com SongSelect)
"Eternal Word" by Linda Holcombe
"Love" by Pierce/Tomlin et al (ccli.com SongSelect)
"Multiply Your Love" by Park (ccli.com SongSelect)
"The Power Of Your Love" by Bullock (ccli.com SongSelect)

Important Items
Reformation Day and Halloween are October 31.

Invocation
P   Dwell with us this day, Son of heaven, and send your Spirit to be in our hearts.
C   Amen.

Confession And Forgiveness
P   Gather at the foot of God's mountain, and we'll confess together our sins in God's presence.
(Silence for reflection)
P   Great law-giver,

C we have failed to even uphold the easiest of commandments and our lives are in desperate need of your intervention. Speak directly to our hearts and cleanse them from the sin that clings closely. Pass your mercy to us for the sake of your Son who died for us, Jesus Christ. Amen.

P Through your faith in Christ, his righteousness cloaks you. Beloved saints, your sins are forgiven in the name of the + Father, Son, and Holy Spirit.

C Amen.

Apostolic Greeting

P Grace and peace be with you, beloved in Christ.

C And also with you.

Prayer Of The Day

A Let us pray. Lord of all,

C we come to you seeking much, and you open your hand in blessing. Form our lives in the direction of your love, and shield our minds from turning away from you. Amen.

Prayers Of The Church

A Let us stand up on behalf of the people of God to ask for God's blessings.

(Silence for reflection)

(After each petition)

A For those who need your care,

C we lift up our voice.

(After final petition)

A Remember your covenant to our ancestors and grant blessings in abundance for all who find themselves in need this day, through Jesus Christ our Lord.

C Amen.

Offertory Prayer

A Let us pray. Holy God,

C your power has been shown across the earth, and the signs are in these gifts we return to you. Help us to let you continue to work through our hands and bless their work so that all we bring back to you may bring new life to those in need. Amen.

Proper Preface

P It is our duty and joy that we offer to you our thanks and praise for the myriad of works you have shown to your people. Your hand guided even when we were rebellious and still continues to this day to guide us back to the communion of all saints, with whom we join in the unending hymn: (Sanctus)

Communion Welcome

P The bread and wine from heaven are given as a gift for you.

Post-Communion Blessing

P As the body and blood of Christ move in your own body, may they strengthen and unite us all in unity of mission.

C **Amen.**

Post-Communion Prayer

A Let us pray. Life-giving Lord,

C **you have fed your family with the true gifts of your sacrifice. Let your passion enflame our hearts that we may reach out in love and service to all whom we meet; in your holy name we pray. Amen.**

Benediction

P May Christ place in your hearts and minds that which was in Christ Jesus: sacrifice, mercy, and love.

C **Amen.**

Dismissal

A Go and tend to the vineyard of the world.

C **We will, ready to greet all in the name of Christ!**

Reformation Sunday

Season After Pentecost Theme: Harvesting

Texts
Jeremiah 31:31-34
Psalm 46
Romans 3:19-28
John 8:31-36

Music Of The Day Traditional Hymns
"A Mighty Fortress Is Our God" (ELW504, GG275, UMH110, H688)
"Faith Of Our Fathers" (ELW813, UMH710, H558)
"The Church's One Foundation" (ELW654, GG321, UMH545, H525)
"As The Grains Of Wheat" (ELW465)
"We Are Marching In The Light" (WOV650, GG853)
"Blest Be The Tie That Binds" (ELW656, GG306, UMH557)

Music Of The Day Contemporary Songs
"Today Is The Day" by Brewster/Baloche (ccli.com SongSelect)
"A Mighty Fortress Is Our God" (ccli.com SongSelect)
"Eternal Word" by Linda Holcombe
"10,000 Reasons" by Myrin/Redman (ccli.com SongSelect)
"A Mighty Fortress" by Nockels (ccli.com SongSelect)
"Communion" by Powell/Avery et al (ccli.com SongSelect)

Important Items
Reformation Day and Halloween are October 31.

To honor the 500th anniversary of the Reformation, several quotes from Martin Luther should be implanted throughout the service, suggestions would be (even though not all of these are direct Luther quotes):

† "Even if I knew that tomorrow the world would go to pieces, I would still plant my apple tree."

† "Music is the art of the prophets and the gift of God."

† "Grant that I may not pray alone with the mouth; help me that I may pray from the depths of my heart."

† "If you want to change the world, pick up your pen and write."

† "Be a sinner and sin boldly, but believe and rejoice in Christ even more boldly."

† "The Bible is alive, it speaks to me; it has feet, it runs after me; it has hands, it lays hold of me."

† "The Bible is the cradle wherein Christ is laid."

† "We are beggars; this is true."

Invocation

P   Dwell in our hearts + Father, Son, and Holy Spirit as we call on you to make all things new.

C   **Amen.**

Confession And Forgiveness

P   Gathered together in the presence of God, let us confess our sins.

(Silence for reflection)

P   Living God,

C   **we are slaves to sin. We have made you into an idol and not worshiped you for who you are, the almighty God who lives and moves. Write your law on our hearts so that we may love and serve you, free from sin, and washed clean in the blood of your Son, our Savior, Jesus Christ. Amen.**

P   The day will surely come when all will know the Lord. Mark this day when God forgives your sins in the name of Jesus Christ, and remembers it no more.

C   **Amen.**

Apostolic Greeting

P   The Lord of hosts grant you grace and peace this day.

C   **Amen.**

Prayer Of The Day

A   Let us pray. Everlasting God,

C   **for us, it has been a long time, but for you it is but a blink of an eye. As we celebrate 500 years of one particular movement, we know that you have breathed life into creation since its inception. Draw us into the company of those who have witnessed to your power to shape not just the church, but the heart of humanity, through the passion of Jesus Christ. Amen.**

Prayers Of The Church

A   Freed in Christ to love and serve our neighbor, let us pray on behalf of those in need.

(Silence for reflection)

(After each petition)

A   Persistent God,

C   **hear our call to you.**

(After final petition)

A   Make us into instruments of your peace to be the healing for the world, through our Lord Jesus Christ.

C   **Amen.**

Offertory Prayer

A Let us pray. Merciful Lord,

C **you have given us all things as gifts: even our salvation and daily bread. For the sake of your creation use these gifts we have returned to teach everyone of your goodness, so that all may partake at the holy feast and know you as Lord. Amen.**

Proper Preface

P It is our delight to sing and pray in thanksgiving for the world your hands have made. You have rescued us from the depths of sin and given us new life — not because of our worth or works, but because that is who you are. Inspire us to faith to believe that we are justified as the saints while we join them in their unending hymn: (Sanctus)

Communion Welcome

P Come, let the body and blood of Christ work in you.

Post-Communion Blessing

P With the bread and wine we have shared, may Christ grow faith in your hearts.

C **Amen.**

Post-Communion Prayer

A Let us pray. Father of all,

C **you tend to our every need. While we don't understand all of what you do for us, let us trust that in this holy meal you have given something different than the world gives: a piece of the holy meal that inspires love in us and for others. Use your mystery to call us into curiosity and seek you in our community. In Jesus' holy name we pray. Amen.**

Benediction

P May God form you into the creation that the world needs. May he continually call to you both in your time of need and in time of abundance. May the + Father, Son, and Holy Spirit grow life all around you.

C **Amen.**

Dismissal

A Go in the name of Christ and tell the good news.

C **Thanks be to God!**

All Saints Sunday

Season After Pentecost Theme: Harvesting

Texts
Revelation 7:9-17
Psalm 34:1-10, 22
1 John 3:1-3
Matthew 5:1-12

Music Of The Day Traditional Hymns

To be sung quietly and meditatively just before the Remembrance of the Saints:
"The Prayers Of The Saints" (Verse 1 & Chorus) (ccli.com SongSelect)

To be sung quietly and meditatively at the end of the Remembrance of the Saints:
"The Prayers Of The Saints" (Verse 2 & Chorus) (ccli.com SongSelect)

"Blest Are They" (ELW728, GG172)
"Shall We Gather At The River" (ELW423, GG375, UMH723)
"As The Grains Of Wheat" (ELW465)
"Jesus Loves Me" (ELW595, GG188, UMH191)
"For All The Saints" (ELW422, GG326, UMH711, H287)

Music Of The Day Contemporary Songs

To be sung quietly and meditatively just before the Remembrance of the Saints:
"The Prayers Of The Saints" (Verse 1 & Chorus) (ccli.com SongSelect)

To be sung quietly and meditatively at the end of the Remembrance of the Saints:
"The Prayers Of The Saints" (Verse 2 & Chorus) (ccli.com SongSelect)

"Did You Feel The Mountains Tremble?" by Smith (ccli.com SongSelect)
"Eternal Word" by Linda Holcombe
"How Can I Keep From Singing?" by Tomlin/Redman/Cash (ccli.com SongSelect)
"Fill My Cup" by Baloche et al (ccli.com SongSelect)
"Breathe" by Barnett (ccli.com SongSelect)

Important Items

Veterans Day is November 11.

Invocation

P We begin in the name of the + Father, Son, and Holy Spirit, God of the living and the dead, who re-unites us with all.

C **Amen.**

Confession And Forgiveness

P As the saints before and saints after, let us confess our sins to God.

(Silence for reflection)

P God our maker and redeemer,

C **forgive us our sins. We have seen those who are in need and turned our heads. We have tried to distance ourselves from neighbors we don't like. We have used words unfitting the children of God. Our sins have caused divisions, hurt souls, and created sadness. Take these burdens and renew our spirit to once again call you Lord. Amen.**

P Salvation belongs to our God and you are saved from all your sins in the name of the + Father, Son, and Holy Spirit.

C **Amen.**

Remembrance Of The Saints

P God of all, we remember with thanksgiving all of those who have lived and died in you:

(Candle 1 is lit, chimes are struck)

   First group of names is read

(Candle 2 is lit, chimes are struck)

   Second group of names is read

(Candle 3 is lit, chimes are struck)

   Third group of names is read

(Candle 4 is lit, chimes are struck)

   Fourth group of names is read

(Candle 5 is lit, chimes are struck)

P Join us together with all of your saints until that time when we shall all sing around your throne throughout all eternity in worship of you.

C **Amen.**

Apostolic Greeting

P Saints of Christ, grace and peace be with you.

C **And also with you.**

Prayer Of The Day

A Let us pray. Almighty and merciful God,

C **we are not worthy of your presence. Yet, you have raised us to glory for the sake of your own goodness. Clothe us in white robes that show your faithfulness can scrub all of our sins and darkness, through Jesus Christ our Savior. Amen.**

Prayers Of The Church

A Strengthened by the witness of the saints who have gone before, let us tend to the work for those in need by asking God's blessing.

(Silence for reflection)

(After each petition)

A Hear our prayer Lord,

C **and send us to serve.**

(After final petition)

A For all those who cross our lips and our hearts this day, we ask your blessing. Give them all that they need and give us the gifts to be the hope in the world, through Jesus Christ our Lord.

C **Amen.**

Offertory Prayer

A Let us pray. Merciful God,

C **you pour blessings out even on those we would consider cursed. For the ways you have blessed us, we give thanks. Inspire in us such generosity to continue to be blessings for your mission and your creation, through our Lord Jesus Christ. Amen.**

Proper Preface

P It is indeed our duty and joy to give thanks and praise to you, holy Father, mighty Lord, life-giving Spirit. You are our rising and falling, our life and death and we owe all to you. With all those saints named today and the billions whose names we will never know, we join together to offer you our voice as we join in their unending hymn. (Sanctus)

Communion Welcome

P This table is for all the saints. Come and be joined at Christ's meal.

Post-Communion Blessing

P May the body and blood of the Lamb wash you and keep you in glory and righteousness all your days.

C **Amen.**

Post-Communion Prayer

A Let us pray. Jesus our Lord,

C **you have shown us a love that is beyond our ability. Help us to share this gift with others and invite them to your feast that they may find your love and be filled, in your holy name we pray. Amen.**

Benediction

P By the lamb of God, you have been washed, fed, and covered in righteousness. Go out with boldness, children of God, to be witnesses of God's glory.

C **Amen.**

Dismissal

A Saints of this time and place, go and be the body of Christ.

C **Amen!**

Proper 27 / Pentecost 23

Season After Pentecost Theme: Harvesting

Texts
Joshua 24:1-3a, 14-25
Psalm 78:1-7
1 Thessalonians 4:13-18
Matthew 25:1-13

Music Of The Day Traditional Hymns
"Holy, Holy, Holy" (ELW413, GG592, UMH64, H362)
"O God Of Mercy, God Of Light" (ELW714)
"When Peace Like A River" (ELW785, LBW346, GG840, UMH377)
"As The Grains Of Wheat" (ELW465)
"Come, Let Us Eat" (ELW491, UMH625)
"Soon and Very Soon" (ELW439, WOV744, GG384, UMH706)

Music Of The Day Contemporary Songs
"Your Grace Is Enough" by Maher (ccli.com SongSelect)
"Indescribable" by Story (ccli.com SongSelect)
"Eternal Word" by Linda Holcombe
"Holy, Holy, Holy" by Morgan (ccli.com SongSelect)
"Where I Belong" by Millard/Graul et al (ccli.com SongSelect)
"Dwell In Your House" by Ewing (ccli.com SongSelect)

Invocation
P   Govern this household Lord and be present with us this day.
C   **Amen.**

Confession And Forgiveness
P   Let us open ourselves to God and confess our sins.
(Silence for reflection)
P   Guiding Father,
C   **we have not eagerly anticipated your return and we have become distracted and made other things into gods and trusted in them. Call us back to you by your words of truth that we may love you and love our neighbor with all sincerity, through Jesus Christ our Lord. Amen.**

P Though God is jealous, God's hand of mercy triumphs. Your sins are forgiven in the name of the + Father, the Son, and the Holy Spirit.

C **Amen.**

Apostolic Greeting

P Brothers and sisters, may the grace and peace of our Lord Jesus Christ be with you all.

C **And also with you.**

Prayer Of The Day

A Let us pray. Lord of all,

C **call this house to serve only you. As we grow weary in waiting for your return focus our energy on proclaiming your kingdom even in the face of evil and darkness. Amen.**

Prayers Of The Church

A Alert to the needs of our neighbors, let us pray for all in the name of Christ.

(Silence for reflection)

(After each petition)

A Hurry to our side, Lord,

C **and answer our prayers.**

(After final petition)

A Pour out your blessings upon your children and continue your reign in this world, through Jesus Christ our Lord.

C **Amen.**

Offertory Prayer

A Let us pray. Gracious Savior,

C **you have granted talents and treasure to all according to their ability. As we return the fruits of those labors to you, build up your kingdom and use us once again to be your witnesses to the world. Amen.**

Proper Preface

P It is right, and it is our joy that we give to you worship and thanks for all the ways you have offered yourself for us. As you continuously bring your kingdom to our hearts again and again we are set free from all that imprisons us. We join together with the saints of every time and place as we join their unending hymn. (Sanctus)

Communion Welcome

P The time has come, and the kingdom is near. Join as one and eat together.

Post-Communion Blessing

P In the body and blood of Jesus Christ, you are forgiven. May they nourish you for the days ahead.

C **Amen.**

Post-Communion Prayer

A Let us pray. Holy God,

C **keep us awake. By your body and blood may you give us endurance to be faithful to the end and to stay alert for any time you show yourself in our lives, through Jesus Christ our Lord. Amen.**

Benediction

P May God protect you, may + Christ encourage you, and may the Holy Spirit lead you forward.

C **Amen.**

Dismissal

A Let us go out, alive and alert!

C **Amen!**

Season After Pentecost Theme: Harvesting

Texts
Judges 4:1-7
Psalm 123
1 Thessalonians 5:1-11
Matthew 25:14-30

Music Of The Day Traditional Hymns
"Here In This Place (Gather Us In)" (ELW532, WOV718, GG401)
"Holy God We Praise Your Name" (ELW414, GG4, UMH79, H366)
"Many And Great, O God" (ELW837, WOV794, GG21, UMH148, H385)
"As The Grains Of Wheat" (ELW465)
"Let Us Break Bread Together" (ELW471, GG525, UMH618, H325)
"This Little Light Of Mine" (ELW677, UMH585)

Music Of The Day Contemporary Songs
"Holy" by Brown (ccli.com SongSelect)
"The Lord Our God" by Stanfill/Ingram (ccli.com SongSelect)
"Eternal Word" by Linda Holcombe
"That's Why We Praise Him" by Walker (ccli.com SongSelect)
"Thank You" by Fielding/Morgan (ccli.com SongSelect)
"One Hope" by Zschech (ccli.com SongSelect)

Important Items
Thanksgiving Day is November 23 in 2017.

Invocation
P   Govern this household Lord, and be present with us this day.
C   Amen.

Confession And Forgiveness
P   Let us open ourselves to God and confess our sins.
(Silence for reflection)
P   Guiding Father,

C we have not eagerly anticipated your return and we have become distracted and made other things into gods and trusted in them. Call us back to you by your words of truth that we may love you and love our neighbor with all sincerity, through Jesus Christ our Lord. Amen.

P Though God is jealous, God's hand of mercy triumphs. Your sins are forgiven in the name of the + Father, the Son, and the Holy Spirit.

C Amen.

Apostolic Greeting

P Brothers and sisters, may the grace and peace of our Lord Jesus Christ be with you all.

C And also with you.

Prayer Of The Day

A Let us pray. Heavenly Lord,

C give us the confidence to believe that you have called us. Whether small or great, our role in your kingdom is significant. Help us to serve to the best of our ability, and to live out our calling in faith, through our Lord and Savior Jesus Christ. Amen.

Prayers Of The Church

A Alert to the needs of our neighbors, let us pray for all in the name of Christ.

(Silence for reflection)

(After each petition)

A Hurry to our side, Lord,

C and answer our prayers.

(After final petition)

A Pour out your blessings upon your children and continue your reign in this world, through Jesus Christ our Lord.

C Amen.

Offertory Prayer

A Let us pray. Gracious Savior,

C you have granted talents and treasure to all according to their ability. As we return the fruits of those labors to you, build up your kingdom and use us once again to be your witnesses to the world. Amen.

Proper Preface

P It is right, and it is our joy that we give to you worship and thanks for all the ways you have offered yourself for us. As you continuously bring your kingdom to our hearts again and again we are set free from all that imprisons us. We join together with the saints of every time and place as we join their unending hymn. (Sanctus)

Communion Welcome

P   The time has come, and the kingdom is near. Join as one and eat together.

Post-Communion Blessing

P   In the body and blood of Jesus Christ, you are forgiven. May they nourish you for the days ahead.

C   **Amen.**

Post-Communion Prayer

A   Let us pray. Holy God,

C   **keep us awake. By your body and blood may you give us endurance to be faithful to the end and to stay alert for any time you show yourself in our lives, through Jesus Christ our Lord. Amen.**

Benediction

P   May God protect you, may + Christ encourage you, and may the Holy Spirit lead you forward.

C   **Amen.**

Dismissal

A   Let us go out, alive and alert!

C   **Amen!**

Christ The King

Season After Pentecost Theme: Harvesting

Texts
Ezekiel 34:11-16, 20-24
Psalm 100
Ephesians 1:15-23
Matthew 25:31-46

Music Of The Day Traditional Hymns
"Come Thou Almighty King" (ELW408, GG2, UMH61, H365)
"Crown Him With Many Crowns" (ELW855, LBW170, GG268, UMH327, H494)
"Beautiful Savior/Fairest Lord Jesus" (ELW838, GG630, H384)
"As The Grains Of Wheat" (ELW465)
"In Christ Alone" by Townend/Getty (ccli.com SongSelect)
"Praise To The Lord The Almighty" (ELW858, GG35, UMH139, H390)

Music Of The Day Contemporary Songs
"The Only Name (Yours Will Be)" by Cowart (ccli.com SongSelect)
"Beautiful One" by Hughes (ccli.com SongSelect)
"Eternal Word" by Linda Holcombe
"In Christ Alone" by Townend/Getty (ccli.com SongSelect)
"We Believe" by Ryan/Fike/Hooper (ccli.com SongSelect)
"Shout To The Lord" by Zschech (ccli.com SongSelect)

Invocation
P   Blessed be the one God + Ruler of the nations, righteous in all his work, and faithful to us.
C   **Amen.**

Confession And Forgiveness
P   Let us gather before the throne of Christ and offer our confession.
(Silence for reflection)
P   Lord of all,
C   **our eyes have been blind to the needs of those around us. We have denied your presence in those who are hungry, thirsty, imprisoned, naked, and sick; have mercy on us. Raise us as you have been raised to new life that we may share your life in all our days ahead. Amen.**

P God has put all things under Christ's feet, and has thus trampled sin and death. By his grace, you are forgiven your sins in the name of the + Father, the Son, and the Holy Spirit.

C **Amen.**

Apostolic Greeting

P Servants of Christ, grace and peace be with you all.

C **And also with you.**

Prayer Of The Day

A Let us pray. Holy Lord,

C **you reign above all, immortal and all powerful yet still desire a relationship with us. Help us not to think so much of ourselves that we ignore your presence in those around us who need care and love. We pray this in your name, to which all of creation bows. Amen.**

Prayers Of The Church

A In service to God most high, let us bring our concerns forward to God.

(Silence for reflection)

Begin each petition of the prayers with:

God, the ruler of the nations...

God, the ruler of all creation...

God, the ruler of the church...

God, the ruler of our whole being...

God, the ruler of both life and death...

(After each petition)

A Our holy king,

C **give us your blessing.**

(After final petition)

A You are the true shepherd and you nourish us and guide us always. So draw our eyes to you that we may follow with our entire lives, through Jesus Christ our Lord.

C **Amen.**

Offertory Prayer

A Let us pray. Gracious God,

C **we humbly return to you to offer what has come from our labors. All that we have is yours, and may you use what we have offered here as well as our very lives for your mission to the world, until the day when our hope becomes truth, through our Lord and Savior Jesus the Christ. Amen.**

Proper Preface

P It is the purpose of our very lives to joyfully offer you our thanks and praise, King of kings and Lord of lords. Your love endures from age to age as your sheep have continually come to recognize. Make our songs joyful as we join with the saints in their unending hymn. (Sanctus)

Communion Welcome

P The royal banquet is prepared, come to your place at the table.

Post-Communion Blessing

P May the body and blood of Jesus Christ keep you in all holiness now and forever.

C **Amen.**

Post-Communion Prayer

A Let us pray. Blessed shepherd,

C **at your table, you have welcomed us and called us brother and sister. Now that we have been fed by your meal, send us to invite others to the feast to end all feasts that all may be one as you and the Father are one. Amen.**

Benediction

P The world is hungry. Feed it. The world needs shelter. Protect it. The world is alone. Befriend it. May + Christ graciously give you all you need to accomplish this mission.

C **Amen.**

Dismissal

A Go in peace, serve your neighbor.

C **Thanks be to God!**

Thanksgiving Day

Season After Pentecost Theme: Harvesting

Texts
Deuteronomy 8:7-18
Psalm 65
2 Corinthians 9:6-15
Luke 17:11-19

Music Of The Day Traditional Hymns
"We Praise You, O God" (ELW870, LBW241, GG612) *Tune: KREMSER*
"We Gather Together" (UMH131, GG336, H433) *Tune: KREMSER*
"Come Ye (You) Thankful People, Come" (ELW693, LBW407, UMH694, GG367, H290)
"For The Beauty Of The Earth" (ELW879, LBW561, UMH92, GG14, H416)
"Praise And Thanksgiving" (ELW689, LBW409)
"As The Grains Of Wheat" (ELW465)
"Now Thank We All Our God" (ELW840, LBW534, UMH102, GG643, H396)

Music Of The Day Contemporary Songs
"Everlasting God" by Brown/Riley (ccli.com SongSelect)
"Thank You Lord" by Moen/Baloche (ccli.com SongSelect)
"10,000 Reasons" by Myrin/Redman (ccli.com SongSelect)
"Indescribable" by Story (ccli.com SongSelect)
"Thank You" by Fielding/Morgan (ccli.com SongSelect)
"God Of Wonders" by Byrd/Hindalong (ccli.com SongSelect)

Invocation
P   Blessed be the God + of all creation who nourishes and provides for all living things.
C   **Amen.**

Litany
P   Let us offer thanks to God this day in remembrance of all we have been given.
P   You provide food when we are famished, give to those who hunger the means to survive.
C   **Thank you, Lord for feeding us.**
P   You provide shelter when we are weary, give to those who weaken a place to rest.
C   **Thank you, Lord for shielding us.**
P   You provide guidance when we are lost, give to those who wander a path home.

C **Thank you, Lord for leading us.**
P You absolve us when we sin, give to those under the burden of sin the gift of abundant life.
C **Thank you, Lord for forgiving us.**
P You hold us close when we turn away, give to those who are alone the peace of your presence.
C **Thank you, Lord for loving us.**
P To you the author of life, we give all our thanks this day!
C **Amen!**

Apostolic Greeting
P Fellow laborers in Christ, grace and peace be with you all.
C **And also with you.**

Prayer Of The Day
A Let us pray. Almighty God,
C **we fail to give thanks enough for all you have done. By your grace open our minds to new appreciation of how you are the living God, breathing life into all of us, through Jesus Christ our Lord. Amen.**

Prayers Of The Church
A In thanks for what has been and hope for what will be, let us approach the throne of God
(Silence for reflection)
(After each petition)
A Merciful Lord,
C **we ask your blessing.**
(After final petition)
A You give and take away in due season. Grant us the voice to declare the good deeds you have done to the ends of the earth, through Jesus Christ our Lord.
C **Amen.**

Offertory Prayer
A Let us pray. Gracious God,
C **the harvest of our labors is from your growth. Take what we return to you and multiply it to grow your kingdom on this earth, through the good news of Jesus Christ. Amen.**

Proper Preface
P It is our joy to return to you what you first gave to us. For every piece of our lives is a mark of your work in us. With all that we are, draw us to worship you, merciful Lord and Savior and join our voices with the saints in their unending hymn:

Communion Welcome
P The harvest feast is prepared, come to the table and eat.

Post-Communion Blessing

P May the body and blood of Jesus Christ fill your lives always.

C **Amen.**

Post-Communion Prayer

A Let us pray. Mighty God,

C **you have fed us again with the new covenant of Christ's body and blood. May it give us the resolve to face the challenges of the world with a strong sense of your presence, and your love in the name of Christ our Lord. Amen.**

Benediction

P You have been made clean by the grace of the + Father, Son, and Holy Spirit. Remember to give thanks to the Lord your God who shall accompany you along the way.

C **Amen.**

Dismissal

A Thanks be to the Lord our God always!

C **Praise God's holy name! Amen!**

Sample Liturgical Replacements For Texts

As explained in the introduction to the Season after Pentecost, these are some suggestions for how to make a portion of the liturgy match one of the favorite Bible verses submitted by members of the congregation. Two examples are given just because they are very popular texts and will likely be submitted.

Psalm 23
Alternative Readings For The Day: Isaiah 40:6-11; Psalm 23; 1 Peter 2:21-25; John 10:14-18

Alternative Prayer Of The Day:
Merciful God, You are the Good Shepherd. You call us, lead us, direct us, feed us, comfort us, and give us everything else we need. At the sound of Your voice, give us the passion to draw near to You so that we may live with You forever in the name of Your Son, our savior, Jesus Christ. Amen.

Alternative Proper Preface:
Holy Shepherd we give You thanks and praise as we should for the ways you have fed us and sheltered us in Your name. In joy we remember the ways You promise to continue to give us all that we need, and indeed even more than we need for the sake of Your own name. And now, with the sheep You have called from every time and place, we join in the unending hymn.

John 3:16
Alternative Readings For The Day: Genesis 22:1-14; Psalm 150; 1 John 4:7-13; John 3:9-17

Alternative Prayer Of The Day:
Lord God, You sent Your only Son to die for us; this is our good news. Help us to trust in Your mercy so that we may communicate to the world Your love for all of Your creation, through Jesus Christ our Lord. Amen.

Alternative Proper Preface:
It is indeed our duty and joy that we should give thanks and praise to You, holy Father. By the gift of Your Son, You have adopted us into Your family and made us one with You for all time. Join us with all the saints who have witnessed to this Good News by singing their eternal hymn.

Eternal Word

Linda Holcombe

Al-le-lu-ia, Al - le-lu-ia! Move our hearts - with Your e-ter-nal word.

Al-le-lu-ia, Al - le-lu-ia! We have come - to You. Praise to - our

God the Fa-ther, Je-sus - the Son of hea-ven; praise to - the Ho-ly Spir-it.

Thanks be - to God! Al-le-lu - ia, Al - le-lu - ia!

Move our hearts - with Your e-ter-nal word. Al-le-lu - ia, Al - le-lu - ia!

We have come - - - to You.

Good News Dawning

Linda Holcombe

Good News dawn-ing, all na-tions will call Him Lord. - Bright Star ris-ing, the Ho-ly One a-dored. Good News dawn-ing, a-wak-en our hearts in praise. - Bright Star ris-ing, car-ols of joy we raise. - We sing from the north and east-ern lands, Dance from the west and south-ern sands, Join hands at the man-ger, full of love. - Where we be-come one. Good News dawn-ing, all na-tions will call Him Lord. - Bright Star ris-ing, the Ho-ly One a-dored. Good News dawn-ing, the Light of the World to come. - Bright Star ris-ing,

231

Jesus, Lamb of God

Linda Holcombe

Je - sus, Je-sus, Lamb of God, Lamb of God. You wash our sins a - way, and place them all be - hind us. Je - sus, Lamb of God, Lamb of God. Your for - give - ness sets us free. Je - sus, Je - sus, Lamb of God, Lamb of God. Your mer - cy is our shel - ter, our - safe - ty from the storm. Je - sus, Lamb of God, Lamb of God. Your mer - cy gives us peace. Je - sus, Je-sus, Lamb of God, Lamb of God. Your lov - ing sac-ri-fice giv-en on the cross. Je - sus, Lamb of God, Lamb of God. Your love - - - gives us new life.

Shout To The North

Good N.E.W.S. Dawning Advent Gospel Welcome

Martin Smith
arr. Linda Holcombe

Church of God, rise up and sing of the com-ing of our King. Hear the

word of God on high; raise the Gos-pel to the sky! - - -

Shout to the north and the south, sing to the east and the west, Je - sus is Sav-ior to all,

Lord of hea-ven and earth.

CPSIA information can be obtained
at www.ICGtesting.com
Printed in the USA
FFOW04n1325121116
29218FF